HOW TO BUILD PLASTIC AIRCRAFT MODELS

SCALE MODELING HANDBOOK NO. 7

BY ROSCOE CREED

	Introduction	page 2
1	Tooling up	page 4
2	Assembling the fuselage	page 9
3	Adding the tail and wings	page 14
4	Choosing and using paints	page 18
5	Applying decal markings	page 25
6	Preparing small parts for assembly	page 28
7	Final assembly techniques	page 31
8	Tricycle landing gear, jets, multiple engines, and biplanes	page 35
9	Detailing and superdetailing	page 41
10	Weathering	page 50
11	Applying gloss and metallic finishes	page 55
12	Displaying your finished models	page 59

All photographs by the author unless otherwise credited.

Editor: Bob Hayden
Copy Editor: Marcia Stern
Art Director: Lawrence Luser
Staff Artist: Wells Marshall

First printing, 1985. Second printing, 1987.
Third printing, 1989. Fourth printing, 1991.

© 1985 by Roscoe R. Creed. All rights reserved. This book may not be reproduced in part or in whole without written permission from the publisher, except in the case of brief quotations used in reviews. Published by Kalmbach Publishing Co., 21027 Crossroads Circle, P. O. Box 1612, Waukesha, WI 53187. Printed in U. S. A. Library of Congress Catalog Card Number 84-052860. ISBN: 0-89024-065-5.

The larger the scale the more detail you can add, but Mike Derderian's Corsair proves that detailing is far from impossible even in 1/72 scale.

Introduction

What happened to the cracks?

Have you ever stood in your local hobby shop, looked into the glass cases at the sleek plastic model airplanes on display there, and asked yourself "What happened to the cracks?" If you have, the question reveals three things about you.

First, it shows you're well enough acquainted with plastic model airplanes to know that many of their major components are made up of halves, and that simply gluing the halves together leaves a crack — a seam, it's called by model builders — that runs down the middle.

Second, the question shows you're interested enough in plastic model airplane construction to want to know why the seams of the models in the display case can no longer be seen.

Third, it shows that even though you may never have built a plastic model airplane (or maybe you've glued together a few and left the seams showing), you'd like to try building one on which the seams don't show, one with a nice paint job, one that looks like a miniature version of the real thing.

If these three things are true of you, then this book you're about to read will tell you what you want to know about building plastic aircraft. The techniques described in the early chapters will tell you not only how to fit, fill, and smooth seams, but how to detail cockpit interiors, straighten warped parts, and ap-

Tom Nelson converted a Monogram 1/72 scale B-52 to this XB-52 version by modifying the nose and tail. The canopy is solid Lucite.

The basic techniques for building realistic aircraft models from plastic kits are easy to learn — and easy to apply. For your first model you'll want to start with a low-wing, tail-dragger monoplane, like this 1/48 scale Ki-100 Tony by Otaki.

ply paint and decals, among other things.

These techniques will help you produce plastic model airplanes that you'll be proud to show off to your family and friends, and that may well end up in your hobby shop's display case to be admired along with the products of your peers. You may even find yourself entering them in model airplane contests in the out-of-the-box category.

The final chapters of this book will take you beyond out-of-the-box model building and into detailing, weathering, and displaying your models. You'll learn how to build models with additional details such as brake lines, radio antennas, and landing lights. With weathering, your models will no longer look like they just rolled off the assembly line. Instead, their paint will appear faded and oil stained; they will look like airplanes that have seen use.

Sound good? Then read on. Keep in mind that reading about model building techniques is the easy part, and don't be discouraged when putting those techniques into practice brings you brief moments of tension and frustration. "Practice" is the key word here: Continued practice, while it may not make you perfect, will make you pretty darn good, and in the end what you learn will reward you with many hours of pleasure as a builder of plastic model airplanes — without cracks!

Painting, decaling, and weathering are among the basic skills you'll learn. Tom Nelson used a combination of hand brushing and airbrushing to produce the striking exhaust-residue pattern on the fuselage of this 1/48 scale Grumman F8F Bearcat.

You don't need an elaborate workshop — here a kitchen table and a borrowed table lamp provide a comfortable and well-lit working area for building models.

1 Tooling up

Learn about the tools you'll need, then buy a kit and have a fit

To build plastic model airplanes you'll need more than an airplane kit and glue, but not a lot more. There are many tools on the market to help you with building your model, and most are relatively inexpensive; for a few others the cost is high. Luckily, for the most part the expensive items are on the "nice to have" list, and the list of necessities is made up of simple, inexpensive tools. The list of basics is short: a hobby knife, cements, seam fillers, sandpapers, masking tape, and paints.

Hobby knives and blades. The most basic of all modeling tools is a good knife. Your best bet is the replaceable-blade type of hobby knife sold by your dealer. You'll probably have to make a choice between a knife with a small, pencil-like handle and a larger one; the smaller version is best for model airplane work. Get a good-quality knife, one that holds the blade securely so it won't twist or fall out while you're working.

Along with the knife, buy a package of extra blades. You'll be appalled at how fast the the edge dulls and the point breaks off. Buy the long, tapered blade shape — the X-acto No. 11, for instance. The No. 11 is the most versatile hobby knife blade, which is probably why it's the one that's in the knife when you buy it.

Sandpaper. When it comes to sandpaper you can save yourself a lot of time, trouble, and money by using only the wet-or-dry variety, the kind used by auto body shops for a smooth, scratch-free finish. Most hobby shops stock it, but if yours doesn't, try a hardware store or an auto parts house. You'll need two grades: 400 and 600. The 400 will do for most rough sanding, and the 600 will provide the finishing touch. One sheet of each will sand several models if you tear the large sheets into smaller pieces. When sanding, occasionally dip the paper into a container of water to remove the plastic residue generated by sanding.

Cement. The most versatile and easiest to use plastic cement is a fast-drying liquid type that doesn't really glue anything, but instead softens the plastic so one part fuses with another. In addition to this, you'll need a small

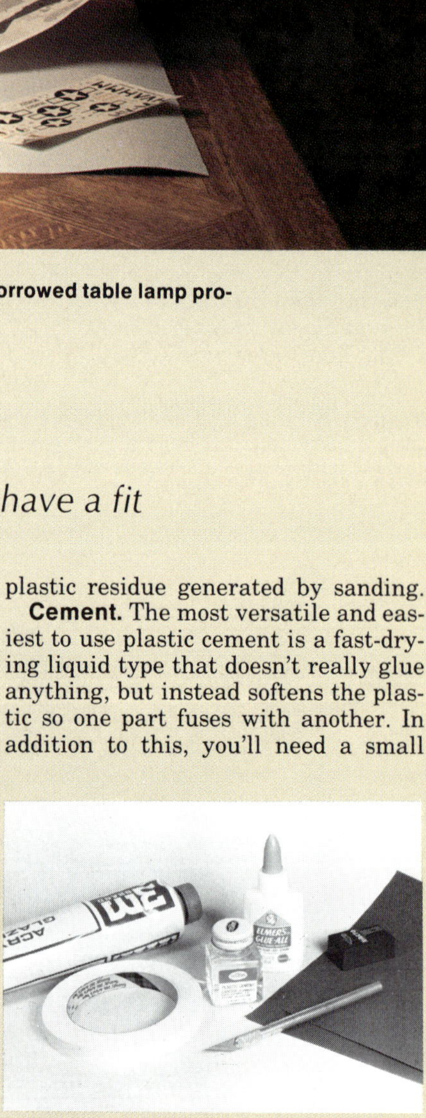

The most basic modeling tools and supplies include a hobby knife, sandpaper, liquid plastic cement and white glue, masking tape, and automotive filler putty.

bottle of white glue for attaching canopies. Other kinds of adhesives will fog and craze clear parts.

Filler putty. Carefully fitting parts and using liquid cement will eliminate the need for most seam filling, but there comes a time and a kit where some sort of seam filler will be called for. Your hobby dealer stocks putty in tubes or bottles to fill seams that can't be hidden any other way. This is not the kind of putty used in windows; it's closer to auto body putty. In fact, if you already envision model building as a long-term endeavor, you can get a lifetime supply of filler putty in a single tube at an auto supply house.

Masking tape. Tape serves a variety of purposes in model building. In addition to performing in its traditional role of covering areas that are not to be painted, it holds parts together while they are being checked for fit and prevents filler putty from being smeared where it's not wanted.

Almost any good tape will do the job, including regular auto masking tape, as long as it has a smooth finish. However, some modelers prefer the thinness of cellophane tape; others prefer drafting or art tapes. Look for the qualities of low tack (less stickiness) — so the tape won't pull off previously applied paint — and pliability — so it will bend around the compound curves you'll encounter.

Modeling paints. Many types and brands of model paint are available. For brush finishing the ideal medium is a water-base paint. It can be applied straight from the bottle — no thinning needed — with any high-quality artist's brush or plastic foam applicator; when dry it lies perfectly flat and shows no brush marks. On the other hand, many fine models are finished with brushed-on oil-base paints, but the techniques for thinning and applying are more difficult to learn than for water-base finishes.

If you choose oil-base paints you'll also need a clear gloss finish to apply over flat colors so decals will adhere properly, and a flat finish to apply over the decals to make the finish dull again. Decals can be applied directly over water-base finishes without the gloss coat; only a flat coat is needed to give the decals a painted-on look. More about paint in Chapter 4.

Brushes. You'll need at least three brushes: one fine point, one medium point, and one chisel point. Buy high-quality red sable artist's brushes that form a sharp point when filled with paint and won't shed hairs on your work. Cleaned and cared for immediately after each use, they will outlast and outperform a handful of cheaper brushes.

A well-lit work space. Once you have the knife, sandpaper, paint, and so forth, the final basic need is a place

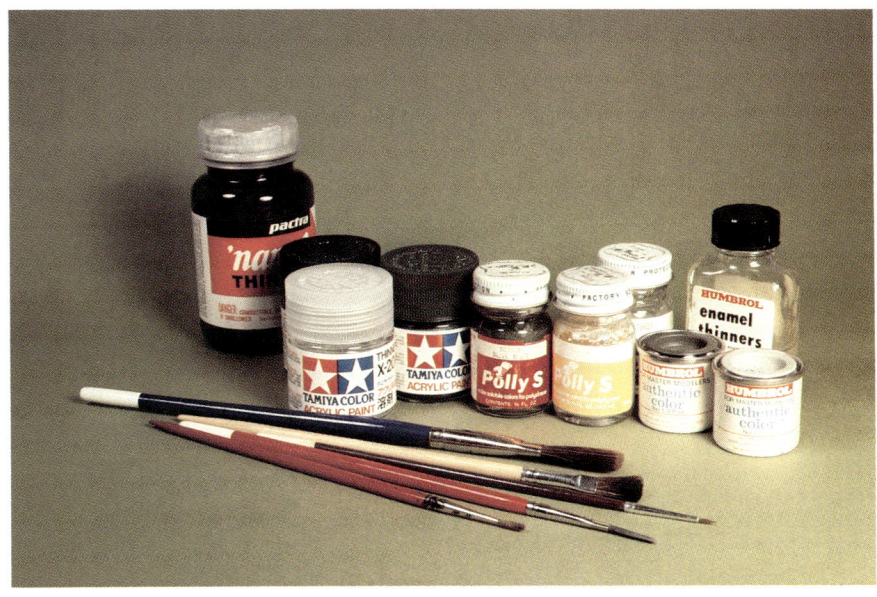

Paints formulated specifically for models are a necessity, as are good brushes. You can choose from a variety of water-base and oil-base paints in appropriate aircraft colors.

to use them. If you have a bench or table of your own, great. If not, the kitchen table may have to suffice when it's off duty from meals. Wherever you work, be sure you have good light. A desk or table lamp moved in close will show up defects in a model that will never be seen under an overhead fixture no matter how good your eyesight — unless of course the model is being examined by a friend or a contest judge.

The "nice to have" tools. Beyond the basic needs are the "nice to have" items, tools that will make building easier and the appearance of your models more professional.

Files. First on the list is a set of miniature files. These reduce sanding time by removing rough edges left by too much cement and by helping to reshape joints that don't match as well as they might. When you buy your files, buy a file card, a little stiff-bristled wire brush for cleaning the plastic out of the file teeth. Properly used (on plastic only), cleaned, and cared for, files are a lifetime investment.

Tweezers. Second on the list are tweezers. Some model airplane parts are too tiny to handle with fingers, so tweezers are the only answer. If you'll have only one pair buy straight tweezers; a second set with points angled at 45 degrees to the handle is also useful.

An airbrush. Third is an airbrush. While it's the most expensive investment you'll make in the hobby, it will also be the most used, outside of your modeling knife. Some modelers believe

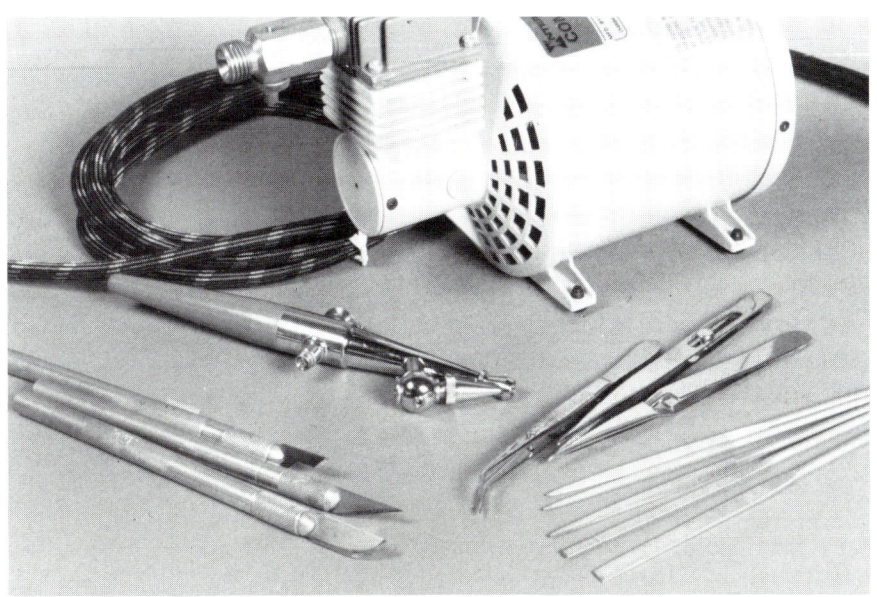

Leading the list of "nice to have" items are extra modeling knives and blades, a set of needle files, two or three types of tweezers, an airbrush, and a compressor. All will make your modeling easier and your results more professional.

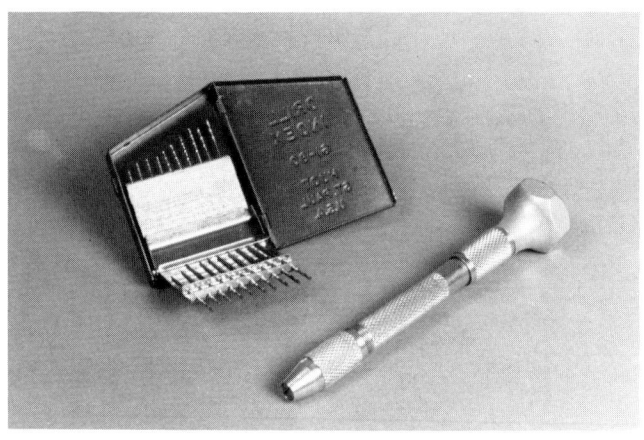
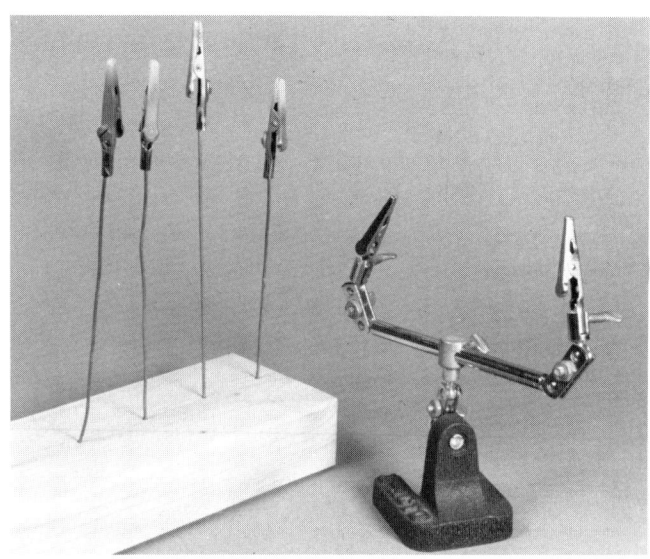

(Right) "Extra hands" holding devices — either factory-produced or homemade — are a big help in assembly and painting. (Above) A pin vise and a set of twist drills (sizes 61 through 80) are indispensable in detailing projects.

that it's actually easier to learn to paint with an airbrush than it is to paint with brushes. Whether that's true or not, the results, once you master basic airbrushing techniques, are much more professional. In fact, there are many color schemes — among them World War Two German and Italian mottled finishes, as well as U. S. and late-war British free-form camouflage schemes — that *must* be applied with an airbrush to look right.

One way to hold down the initial cost of an airbrush outfit is to buy only the airbrush and cans of propellant, thereby eliminating the expense of an air compressor. But if you use the airbrush much (and you will), you'll find the cost of propellant cans will soon amount to the price of a good compressor.

More knives. A couple of extra modeling knives are handy, especially ones with different blade shapes. The round-end No. 10 blade and the short-edged No. 16, which is easier to control than a No. 11 in some situations, are well worth having.

"Extra hands." These small, movable alligator clips fastened to a handle and then to a base are excellent for holding small parts while cementing or painting. The devices are available commercially through your hobby shop, or you can make your own.

Buy a handful of alligator clips at an electronics store, attach them to 6"-long stiff wire handles, drill holes a few inches apart in a piece of scrap lumber, and drop the handles in. The clips grip small parts; the handles allow you to turn them in any direction for painting with brush or airbrush without painting your fingers; the board holds the painted pieces upright and apart while they dry.

Pin vise and drills. Later on, when you get into detailing, you'll find a pin vise and a set of small drills indispensable for cleaning out openings and adding extra parts such as antennas and brake lines.

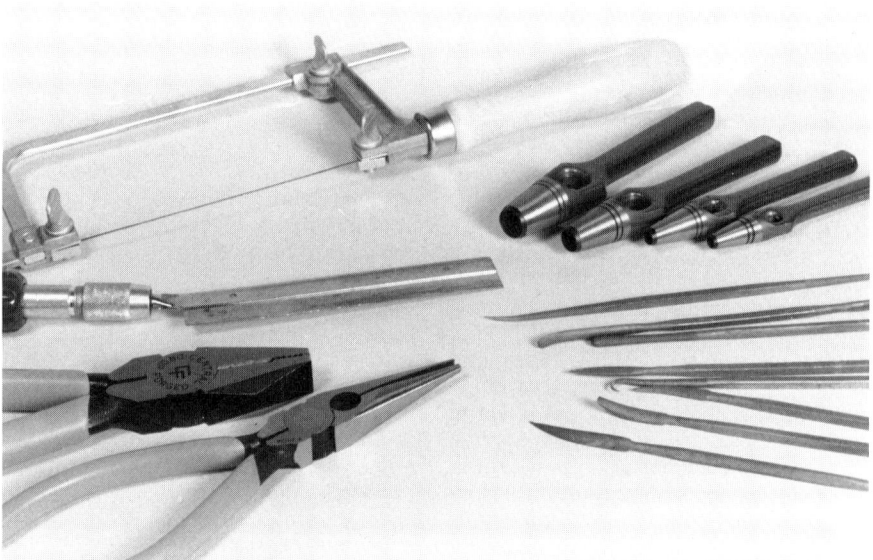

More of those "nice to have" tools: (Above) Pliers, saws, punches, and riffler files simplify model building and aid in adding details. (Below) A hand-held motor tool for grinding and polishing can also come in handy as a miniature lathe.

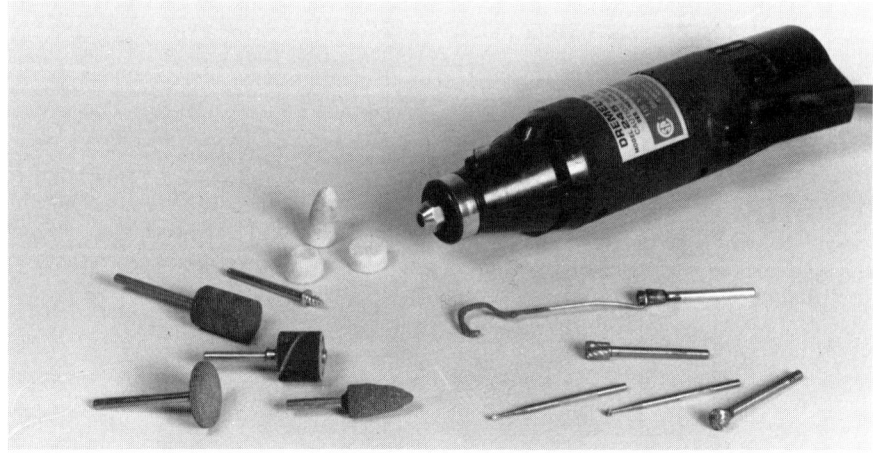

Pliers. Small pliers — side cutters, flat nose, and needle nose — are handy for cutting and forming wire. The side cutters can also be used to remove kit parts from their molding trees, eliminating the possibility of breaking off the stump down inside the part itself, then having to putty up the cavity.

Saws. A thin-bladed razor saw and a jeweler's saw that looks like a miniature coping saw are necessities for detailing and modifying. You'll need them where parts are to be removed and replaced in different positions — control surfaces, for instance — or where one part is to be replaced with another to alter the version of an aircraft — for example, changing the rudder on a Catalina I to make it a Catalina V.

Riffler files. An airbrush and compressor may be the most expensive investment you'll make in your hobby, but there are others that can eat up some cash, too. The most worthwhile of these is a set of riffler files. These have small heads, in a variety of shapes, set at an angle to a long handle. The angled heads and unusual shapes allow access to hard-to-reach areas, and you can reshape oversize fillets and the like without the danger of end gouging, as is likely with a straight file.

Punches. A set of leather punches will allow you to cut perfect circles from masking tape or thin plastic sheet. These are a godsend when painting Japanese hinomarus or manufacturing wheel hubs.

A motor tool. A motor tool with an assortment of bits and grinders can remove plastic much faster than filing or sanding. In fact, it works so fast that you can easily remove more material than you intended, so practice on scrap before you grind away on a high-priced kit. In some instances a motor tool can serve as a miniature lathe for shaping parts that are to be perfectly round.

And so forth. The "nice to have" list is endless; these are only the major items. Eventually you may want to add scribers, a bench vise, various types of cement, polishes, a vacuum-forming machine — whatever suits your desires and your purse.

If your hobby budget permits, you may want to move some of the "nice to have" tools onto your "necessities" list. But don't go the other way: Don't try to omit any of the basic items, because you can't turn out a good out-of-the-box model without them.

We buy a kit and have a fit. We now embark on a walk-through that will show you how to build an out-of-the-box plastic scale aircraft, all the way from buying the kit to setting the finished product on the shelf. To keep it simple, three planes, a North American P-51 Mustang, a Mitsubishi Zero, and a Republic P-47 Thunderbolt — all World War Two single-engine, propeller-driven, low-wing "tail draggers" — will be used to illustrate basic assembly and painting techniques.

Why choose one of these? Simplicity. In either 1/72 or 1/48 scale these models have relatively few parts to worry about. When the parts are assembled the model is easy to paint, since each of these three aircraft had only a two-color camouflage scheme — one color on the top, another on the bottom.

For your first model, choose a single-engine, low-wing, tail-dragger monoplane. This type of aircraft has relatively few parts and is easy to build in any scale.

Choosing a small-scale kit to start with also keeps the cost low, an important consideration. It's far less discouraging to replace an inexpensive kit and start over if disaster should befall your early attempts.

Once you've built a few single-engine monoplanes and have the hang of it, you can proceed to jets, multiengine aircraft, planes with tricycle landing gear, biplanes, and kits in larger scales with lots of parts.

The in-store check. Once you've selected a kit and paid for it, open the box while you're still in the store (dealers frown on kits being opened before they're paid for). Check the canopy to see if it has been scratched, and examine the sprue trees — the frames the parts are attached to — for stumps. If you find any, something was broken off when the plastic was removed from the mold or when the kit was packaged. With luck you'll find the loose part in a corner of the box. Also check for parts that are broken or didn't fill out in the mold.

If you find that parts are missing or damaged, quietly inform the dealer. He should be glad to improve customer relations by trading a good kit for bad.

Usually, however, the in-store examination will reveal that you have an acceptable kit (manufacturers and their inspectors are pretty good today), one rich enough in detail to be built out of the box into a beautiful model. So you head for home with your airplane, along with the tools and materials from your "necessary" list that you don't already have, and prepare for the next step.

(Above) Start by cutting the model's major parts off the sprue trees and taping them together for a trial fit. (Below) Trial fit canopy parts, too, to eliminate problems later on.

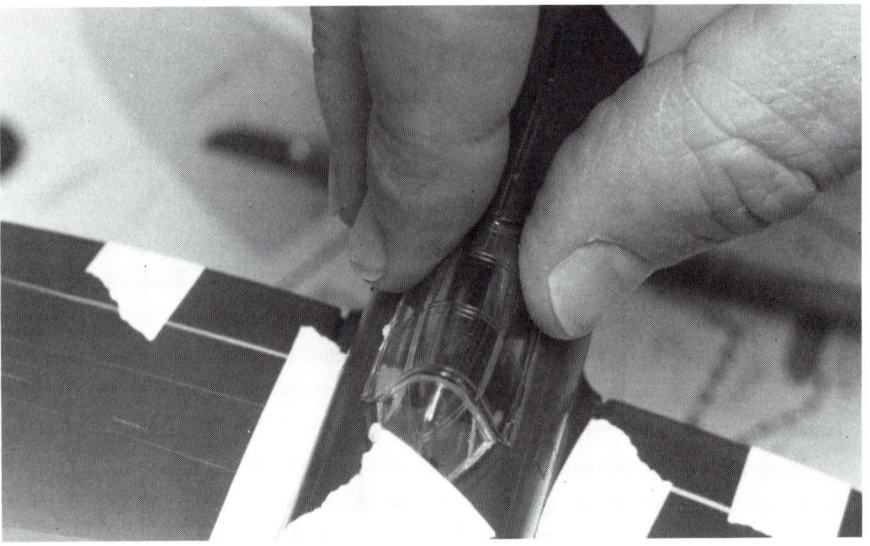

Reading the instructions. Upon arriving home the first step is to read the kit instructions. Don't fall into the "when all else fails, then read the instructions" trap; instead, get into the habit of familiarizing yourself with the kit designer's ideas on how the model should go together. Sometimes the designer won't follow the usual patterns for assembly, and some things must be done his way. It's good to know his thinking before you reach the "I wonder where this part goes" stage late in assembly, when you'll have to choose between discarding the part or preparing for emergency surgery on the model.

Trial fitting parts. Instructions now in mind, you're ready to trial fit the major parts. Use your knife to cut the big parts — fuselage halves, wing and tail surfaces, engine cowling, whatever — from the sprue trees. Don't break the parts off, because doing so could damage them or leave ugly holes that would have to be filled later. Cut on a scrap piece of wood or cardboard. Don't cut off all the parts, certainly not the small ones. Leaving small parts on the trees helps with identification and prevents them from being lost.

Using short pieces of masking tape here and there, put the major components together. Right away you'll begin to see what the model actually looks like. Right off the bat you may also find that some of the major components won't go together because of oversize assembly tabs or undersize receiving slots, and a little work with the knife may be required even before you can complete the trial fitting. But read the instructions again before you cut.

Check the fit of seams and butt joints for gaps and offsets that must be reckoned with before you're ready to lay on the cement. Check the fit of major clear parts, too — an ill-fitting canopy can cause a lot of grief, simply because the techniques for solving problems with clear parts are difficult and time consuming. Clear parts are more brittle than other plastic; they crack easily when squeezed, cut, filed, or sanded. They craze and fog from cement. They scratch easily, and although scratches can be sanded and polished out, clear parts never look quite factory fresh after reworking.

A spritual lift! All in all, trial fitting your kit is an uplifting experience. In your mind's eye you can look past all that monochrome plastic and see the completed aircraft in the proper color scheme and markings, ready for flight. In the quiet of your work area you may even perform a few zooms with your taped-together collection of parts, accompanied by the appropriate sound effects.

Scrub-a-dub-dub! Cleaning the kit parts with dishwashing detergent and an old toothbrush removes mold lubricants and finger oils, ensuring strong glue joints and good paint jobs.

2 Assembling the fuselage

Body building exercises

Now the fun of fitting is over, the euphoria gone. It's time to get serious about permanently joining some parts. The place to start is at the heart of things: with the fuselage.

Washing the parts. First, dismantle your taped-together plane and head for the sink to give everything a bath. This includes the major components you've been working with, as well as the small parts still on the sprue trees.

Soak the parts for about ten minutes in warm water and a little dishwashing detergent, swishing them around occasionally and brushing them with an old soft toothbrush to remove the oily lubricant used in the molding process. This mold lubricant can prevent cement from fusing and paint from sticking, so get rid of it now while you're thinking about it.

Rinse the kit pieces in clear water until all the detergent bubbles are gone. Then dry the parts — a combination of shaking and air drying is best.

Flat-sanding seams. Once the parts are washed, rinsed, and dried, put a big piece of sandpaper on a flat surface and rub the seam edges of the fuselage halves on it. This operation accomplishes two things: It contributes to an absolutely perfect fit along the seams by removing mold marks, excess plastic, and minor warps, and it gives the cement a slightly roughened surface to work with when it's time to cement the fuselage halves together.

Sanding also removes the little alignment pins that the manufacturer provided, but the trade-off in seam fit usually is worth the sacrifice in ease of alignment.

A word of caution: If your model has appendages molded into one fuselage half that extend into the other, such as tail wheels or oil coolers, you will only be able to flat-sand the edges of the receiving fuselage half using this technique. Smooth the edges of the half with the appendages with a sanding block made by wrapping sandpaper around a small scrap of wood.

Edge sanding done, use your hobby knife to scrape away mold marks and flash (the extra plastic that sometimes squeezes out at the edge of a mold and

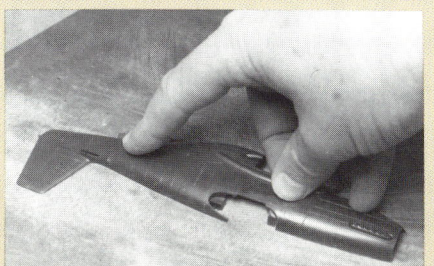 

(Left) Flat-sand the mating surfaces of the fuselage parts for a good fit and good cement adhesion. (Right) Use a sanding block to do the same for parts that have raised areas.

Use the back of the hobby knife blade, not the sharp cutting edge, to scrape away "flash" (excess plastic left by the mold the model was made in).

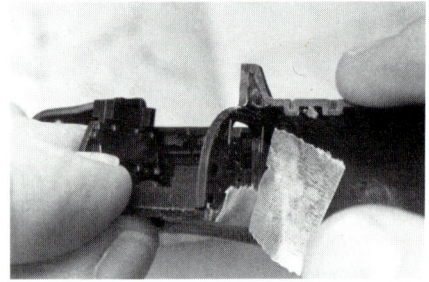

Cockpit parts must be trial-fitted to make sure that the fuselage halves will close over them. Note the flat-sanded edges of the fuselage half shown here.

Wherever possible, true the edges of clear canopy parts with a sanding block.

(Top) Washing and rinsing small parts in a strainer will keep them from being lost down the drain. (Center) Cockpit parts to be painted on one side can be held by sticking them to loops of masking tape on a board. (Above) Parts to be painted on both sides can be gripped by an attaching lug in a "helping hands" clip.

forms an unwanted fringe on the edge of a part). You may find flash around the cockpit, air intakes, oil coolers, and other openings. It may be hard to see now, but will show up with shocking clarity after painting. Use the back edge of the knife blade to scrape, not the sharp one. You merely want to smooth the rough spots, not cut new channels. Check closely; you may have left scrape marks that need to be sanded off.

Fitting the canopy. Now tape the fuselage halves together again, align them carefully, and test fit the clear parts. If the fit is not good, either the edges of the fuselage openings or the clear parts need sanding. When working with a clear part cover all but the area to be sanded with masking tape to prevent scratches.

If the canopy fits against the fuselage at the back and bottom with butt joints, such as those found on an early model Mustang, these must be carefully sanded so they come out straight and square. Keep your sandpaper rigid and straight by wrapping it around a block of wood.

Bubble canopies can sometimes be fitted by holding a piece of sandpaper around the fuselage and sliding the canopy back and forth, giving the canopy the exact contour of the fuselage. But usually the headrest is in the way, and the sanding must be done with the sandpaper wrapped around a section of dowel of appropriate diameter.

Go slowly. Removing too much plastic can create more problems than you solve, such as offsets at the back and bottom of a butt-jointed canopy. It's better to settle for a less-than-perfect fit in some areas in favor of good alignment overall, and to plan to fill the gaps later with white glue.

Fitting the cockpit interior. Now cut the major cockpit interior parts from the trees — instrument panel, floor, rear bulkhead, if any — and scrape the edges as you did the fuselage openings. Untape the fuselage halves and check the fit of the cockpit parts by taping them in one half and closing the other half over them. A floor or instrument panel that's too wide can destroy the perfect fit of your fuselage seams simply by holding them apart. Sand the edges of the cockpit parts to relieve that situation if needed.

Most models have cockpit sidewalls molded into the fuselage halves, but some have sidewalls molded separately, so the cockpit forms a neat little capsule when completed. Take these sidewalls into consideration when test fitting the cockpit parts.

Now remove the rest of the small parts — control stick, seat, rudder pedals — one at a time from the sprues, scrape and sand away mold marks and flash, and put them in a container so you can find them when you need them.

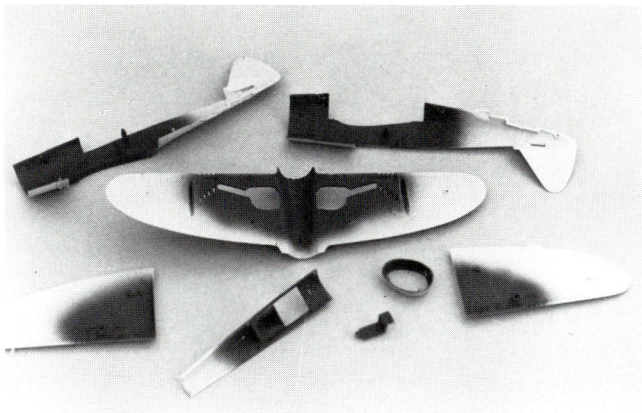 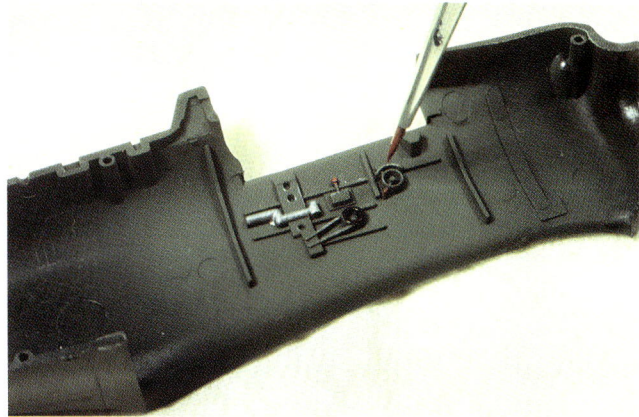

(Left) If the same color, paint the insides of engine cowlings, air scoops, and wheel wells along with the cockpit interior (photo by Bob Angel). (Right) Hand paint cockpit details — throttle quadrants, radios, switch boxes — when the basic color is dry.

Painting the cockpit interior. By now you may be wondering whether you should paint something, and there's no reason why you shouldn't. You've washed off the mold lubricant, scraped off the flash and mold marks, and you know all the large parts fit. You should have the right colors and types of paint for your plane's interior.

Begin by washing the cockpit parts and the inside of the fuselage halves again to remove oily fingerprints, dust, and scraping residue. Tiny cockpit parts can easily go down the drain, so put them in a tea strainer or small sieve for gentle washing, rinsing, and drying.

When all parts are dry — make sure there are no little hidden beads of water to make bubbles under the paint — anchor the small parts that need paint only on one side to stiff cardboard or scrap wood. Use tape formed into loops with the sticky side out, or double-stick tape if you have it. Group the parts by the colors they will be painted.

Parts that need paint on both sides must be painted in two steps unless you have the "extra hands" described in Chapter 1. With these you can grip the part by a joint pin or other appendage that will be hidden after assembly, then paint all sides at once. Make sure the clip has a good grip on the part. The pressure from either hand brushing or airbrushing can make small parts pop out of the clip, to be lost forever in the carpet or some inaccessible corner.

Paint the inside of the fuselage halves either before or after the small interior parts, depending on your mood. Once the basic color is dry, hand paint the small molded-in components — radios, switch boxes, oxygen regulators, hoses, throttle quadrants, and the like — which usually come in black, but could be other colors. Check the instruction sheet.

Also paint the interiors of open air scoops, engine cowlings (if part of the fuselage), and the like in the proper colors. Here again, refer to the kit instructions.

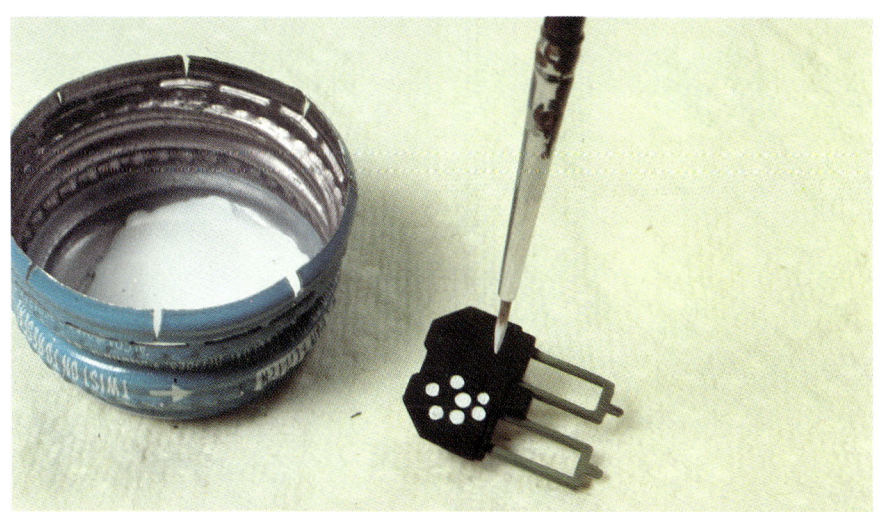

(Top) If your kit came with decals for the instrument panels, apply a coat of clear gloss finish over the flat color coat so the decal film will adhere properly. (For more detailed information on decals, see Chapter 5.) (Above) Painting an instrument panel with raised, molded-in detail is easy: Place a dot of paint in the center of each instrument dial face and let the paint spread to fill the molded outline.

Finishing the instrument panel. If your kit provides a decal for the instrument panel you can apply it with no further ado if you painted the panel with water-base paint. If you used flat oil-base paint, first apply a coat of clear gloss finish to the panel. Let the gloss dry, apply the decal, let it dry, wash off the excess decal glue, then apply a coat of flat finish over the gloss.

(Above) Assemble the cockpit by applying liquid cement with a brush or drafting pen to the backs and undersides of the joints. (Right) The completed cockpit tub for a Monogram 1/48 scale Thunderbolt, including a hand-painted instrument panel.

The whole procedure sounds unnecessary since you started out with a flat finish in the first place, but it's the only way to get a decal to lie down and stay there.

On the other hand, the panel may have the instruments molded in and simply require painting. Black panels with black instruments — like those in Mustangs and Zeros — are easy to do. First paint everything flat black. Then, holding a white lead pencil sideways, rub the lead over the instruments, letting it touch only the raised details. Finally, put a drop of clear gloss finish, liquid floor wax, or polyurethane varnish on each instrument to simulate glass covers.

The Thunderbolt has white instruments on a black panel, however. Paint the panel black, then, when dry, put a dot of white in the center of each instrument and let it spread to fill the outline. Bring out the raised portions of the instruments by "dry brushing": Dip a brush in black paint, brush it dry on a tissue or cardboard scrap, then rub the edges of the brush across the instruments as you did with the white pencil on black instruments. Simulate the glass covers with gloss finish, wax, or varnish.

Assembling the cockpit. With all parts painted and the instrument panel completed, you're ready to assemble the interior. Thanks to your earlier fitting there's hardly anything to it. Scrape away paint from areas to be cemented and follow the manufacturer's instructions and your intuition. In the smaller scales most cockpit interiors build up from the floor, forming a module that slips into one fuselage half.

You're now ready to experience the joys of working with liquid cement. Rarely will you put liquid cement on each piece to be joined and press them together, as you would with tube glue. Instead, you take advantage of a phenomenon known as "capillary attraction." Simply hold together the two pieces to be joined and touch the seam with the tip of a small brush dipped in liquid cement. Capillary attraction pulls the cement out of the brush and into the seam, where it softens and fuses the parts, quickly forming a bond.

Apply cement from the bottom of the floor and the backs of the bulkheads and instrument panels as you build the cockpit module. Later, when you install the cockpit in the fuselage, do the same. If cement is applied to the front surfaces of painted parts it can act as paint remover, and at the least the cement leaves circles that require touching up.

Now set the cockpit module aside overnight while the softened plastic hardens. Then, in the light of a new day, fit the module inside the fuselage half, cement, and again let the joints set overnight.

When all interior parts are in place, touch up the spots where you scraped off too much paint prior to cementing, take one last look around to make sure you haven't left anything out, then test fit the second fuselage half again. This last check, using tape, will tell you whether or not your painstakingly fit-

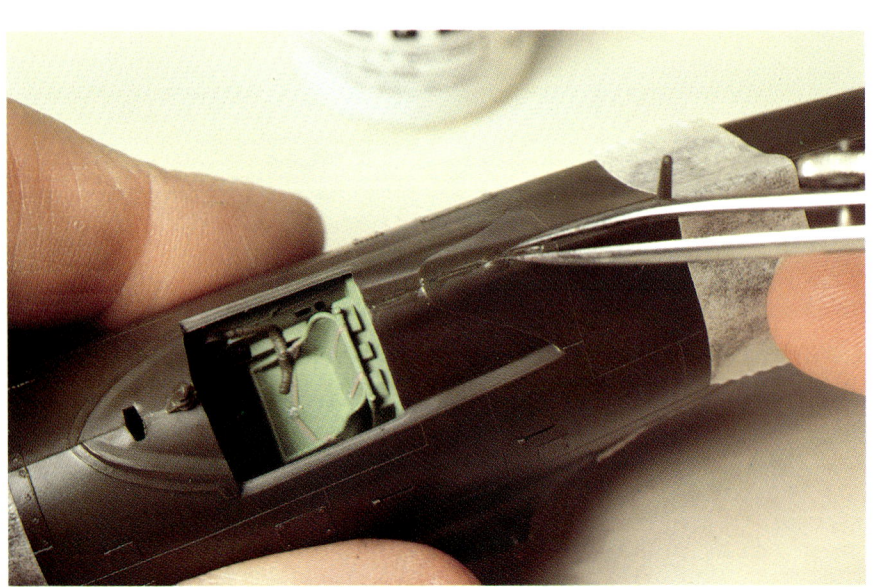 

(Left) Once the cockpit components have been installed, apply liquid cement to the seams where the fuselage halves meet. (Above) When the cement has dried and the plastic has hardened, smooth the fuselage seams with a sanding block.

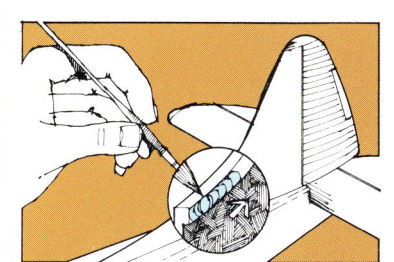

To bond plastic parts, hold them together and touch a brush dipped in liquid cement to the seam. Capillary attraction will pull the cement out of the brush and into the seam, spreading it as far as the quantity allows. Continue applying cement until the seam is filled.

CEMENTING WITH LIQUID CEMENT

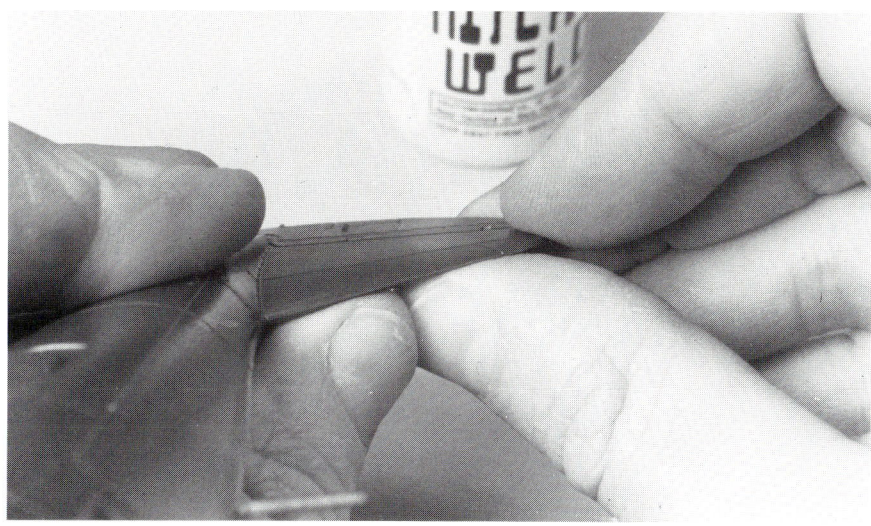

Molded-in vertical fins that are warped can be straightened during assembly by bending them against the warp while the cement sets.

ted fuselage seams still mate. If they do, you're ready to close up.

Assembling the fuselage halves. Scrape away excess paint from the fuselage seams, align them, lightly hold the halves together, and apply cement to the seam just as you did to the cockpit interior parts. Capillary attraction will make the cement flow into the seams, creating a strong bond. But beware — the same attraction will also cause the cement to flow with equal ease under your fingers, making your fingerprints a permanent part of the exterior detail. Keep your fingers well back from the seams to prevent this.

Since you no longer have those little alignment pins to depend on, you must hold each cemented section in place for a few moments until the softened plastic hardens enough to hold its position. As you gently press the fuselage halves together, softened plastic may ooze up out of the seam. This is good; it means the seam is filled. Don't worry about this bead of excess plastic now; you can sand it off later after it hardens.

Many single-engine fighters in the smaller scales have the vertical tail fin molded into one or both of the fuselage halves. If the fin also is in halves, these should be cemented together along with the fuselage. Watch for warps. These are easy to correct, since tail fin halves are thin and pliable. Simply hold the halves in alignment with the fuselage center line while you apply cement to the edges.

Once all the fuselage and fin seams are cemented and maintain their alignment, set the unit aside for the joints to harden overnight. Next day, cover the cockpit opening with tape to keep out sanding dust, then sand off the excess plastic along the seams, using a sand-

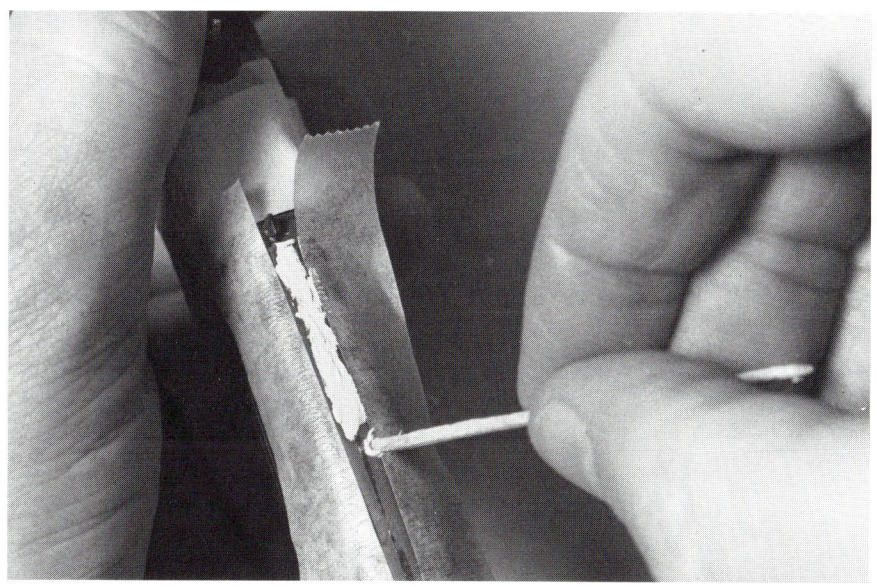

If seam filling is required on the fuselage joints, mask the area with tape to protect adjacent detail, then apply filler putty sparingly with a toothpick or small dowel.

ing block wherever possible. Proceed gently so the little bubbles in the plastic bead don't break off. If they do, the break will probably occur below the surface, leaving pits that will have to be puttied later.

Thanks to your earlier flat-sanding of fuselage joints you should find little need for putty to fill the seams. If you do, place masking tape alongside the seam, back from the edge about $1/16"$ on either side, and apply putty sparingly with a toothpick or small dowel cut at an angle. The tape keeps putty out of areas where it isn't needed, and pre-

vents sanding away molded-in detail when smoothing the putty.

Sand the putty when dry, using your sanding block. Repeat the procedure until all gaps and pits are filled.

Now the seams are sealed. So is the fate of your fuselage. This is one of those satisfying moments in modeling — the fuselage has some weight now, and a feeling of quality to it. When you remove the tape covering the cockpit and look in, it looks like a miniature airplane inside, just as you wanted. You can smile and take a deep breath. You're off to a good start.

3 Adding the tail and wings

Bringing up the rear, and winging it

When you've tired of smiling at your fuselage, tape over the openings to keep out dust, fingers, and overspray, and move on to cleaning up and attaching the tail surfaces. The reason for doing so now: While your bird is yet wingless, you can reach the tail surface joints easily from any direction.

If the vertical fin of your Thunderbolt, Mustang, or Zero is molded as part of the fuselage halves — most are — you're already partway home. You cemented the fin halves together along with the fuselage, straightening warps in the fin as you moved along.

Straightening warped solid tail surfaces. Most Zero, Thunderbolt, and Mustang models in the smaller scales have horizontal stabilizers that are molded solid, and a few have separate solid vertical fins. These parts usually don't warp, but anything is possible in model building. If you find a solid warped tail surface, you'll have to resort to heat treating to straighten it.

Here's how: Heat a pan of water to 180 degrees on the kitchen stove, dunk the warped part in it for a few seconds — try three to five for starters — then remove the part and bend it against the warp until it cools. Continue to dunk, bend, and cool until the part remains straight.

The thinner the part, the less heat required to soften it. All tail surface parts are thin at trailing edges and tips, so these areas will soften first. Don't touch the edges while bending; instead, apply pressure only at the thickest section of the chord or you may end up with a wavy trailing edge or bent tip. Too much heat in one dunking and the edges may end up wavy on their own. (This provides you with a golden opportunity to start over with another kit.)

Once the stabilizers are straightened, use your sanding block to remove excess plastic and mold marks from the edges. Aren't you glad you haven't yet attached these parts to the fuselage? Unattached, you can turn them in any direction and easily reach any edge. And you can sand the edges without running the risk of cracking a carefully engineered root-fuselage seam, as you would if the parts had been attached before cleanup.

Fitting tail surfaces. Straightening done and edges sanded to a paint-ready state, refit the tail surfaces to the fuselage and check the quality of the root joints, where the parts meet. If you find gaps and your model has tail surfaces that attach to the fuselage with butt joints, eliminate or reduce the gaps by going over the tail surface roots with a sanding block.

If the tail surfaces attach to rounded fillet roots molded into the fuselage, sand both the fuselage roots and the tail surface roots until they match. Use a sanding block or sandpaper wrapped around a dowel, depending on whether the roots are straight or curved. On either type of root, if the gaps are too great to be eliminated you'll have to fill them with putty later.

Filleted roots present an additional problem: You may find a variance in thickness between them and the tail surface root. This can be as much as several scale inches, which, if not corrected, results in an ugly, offset joint. Usually it's the fillet root on the fuselage that's too thick, and you can sand it down with paper wrapped around a small dowel or paintbrush handle until it matches the thickness of the fin or stabilizer.

If the fillet root is thinner than the tail surface root, your best bet is to build up the fillet with putty after the two are cemented together.

Aligning and attaching the tail surfaces. Now, with the tail surfaces fitted to the fuselage to the best of your ability, start making them permanent. Begin with the vertical fin, if it is a separate part. Sighting from the front, align the fin with the vertical center line of the fuselage and apply cement to the root seam. Check and recheck alignment while the joint hardens.

When the fin joint has solidified, at-

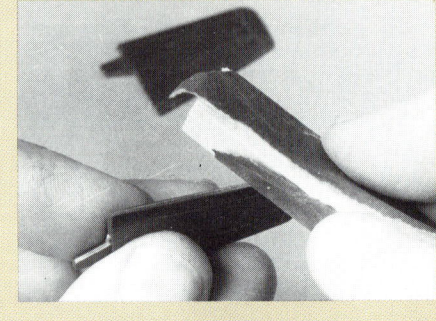

To straighten a warped part, dunk it in 180-degree water for a few seconds, then bend against the warp and hold the part straight until it cools.

(Top) Use a sanding block to remove mold marks and flash from fins and stabilizers, and (above) to flat-sand tail surface root joints for a flush fit.

Filleted root joints that have been puttied should be sanded smooth with sandpaper wrapped around a round object such as a small dowel or paintbrush handle. Be sure to mask the surrounding areas to prevent scratching the detail.

tach the horizontal stabilizers, sighting carefully to ensure that each is 90 degrees to the fin. Don't let the taper from root to tip fool you — the stabilizers may look droopy when they're not. Check by sighting along the center line, and for a double check, turn the fuselage 90 degrees so the horizontal stabilizers are vertical. This way it's easier to see the center line through the horizontal stabilizers. Keep the stabilizers vertical while cementing, or hold them in alignment with tape strung from the tips to the top of the vertical fin. Set the assembly aside while the joints harden.

Once the joints have set, sand away excess plastic and see if you have a perfect joint. If your fitting and cementing was good, you won't have any seams to putty. Few people are that skilled, however. Apply putty as needed, using the taping-and-toothpick technique described in Chapter 2 for fuselage seams, and sand when dry.

Now the tail parts have set, their alignment is good, and the seams are filled. You can sit back, drink something cold (or hot, depending on the season), and contemplate the beauty of the wingless dodo you have just produced.

Winging it. Set the completed fuselage and tail assembly aside where it won't be knocked off the workbench in a frenzy of activity, and get ready to tackle the next major effort: adding wings.

Wings come in two basic configurations for small-scale Zeros, Mustangs, and Thunderbolts: individual left and right wings that butt against the fuselage or fuselage fillets, and single-part wings, the center portion of which is actually part of the fuselage. Either type can be molded solid or in halves.

Since wings are long and thin they are more susceptible to warping than any other part of the plane. You probably discovered this in your trial fitting session, when you sighted down the leading and trailing edges of the taped-together parts. Occasionally the wings are perfect, but more often you'll find gull or inverted-gull wings on a plane that's supposed to have straight ones.

Don't despair. Wing warps are no more difficult to solve than the ones you dealt with on the tail surfaces — it's the same problem, just larger parts.

Straightening and attaching solid wings. Warps in solid-molded wings can be eliminated using the same hot-water treatment described above for solid tail surfaces.

With one exception, the procedure for attaching solid, butt-jointed wings is the same as for attaching horizontal stabilizers: Edge sand the wings to remove mold marks, then sand the roots until they fit, matching up the fillets, if any, to the wing roots. But before you cement the wings in place, that one exception must be dealt with. It's the matter of dihedral — the rise in the wings from root to tip.

The importance of having equal dihedral angles for both wings goes beyond simple accuracy to scale. Even the slightest difference in angle will give your model a twisted appearance when viewed head on. The twist can also be noticeable when the model is completed and sitting on its landing gear.

It's relatively easy to establish dihedral angles for solid-molded wings that butt against the fuselage or fillets. Simply plug the alignment tabs — usually provided on butt-jointed wings — into the fuselage slots. Then, holding the wings tightly against the fuselage or fillets, sight along the model from nose to tail. The dihedral angle should be the same for both wings, and should match the front-view drawing in the instructions.

A little sanding may be needed on

(Top) Turn horizontal stabilizers vertical to double-check their alignment while sighting along the fuselage. (Above) Hold the stabilizers in place with masking tape while the cement dries.

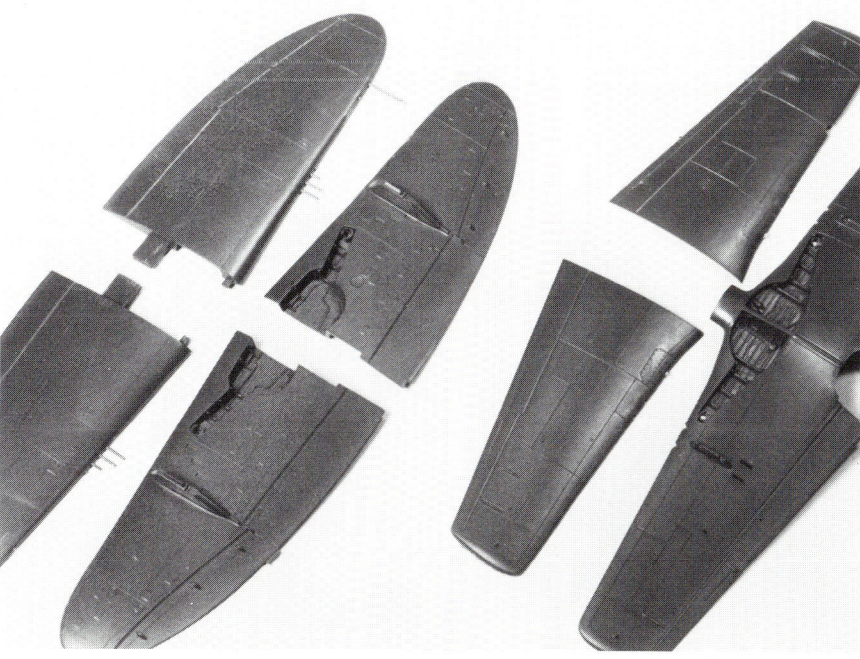

Most wings are molded either in four parts (at left in photo) or three parts (right), with the center portion of the bottom part forming a section of the fuselage.

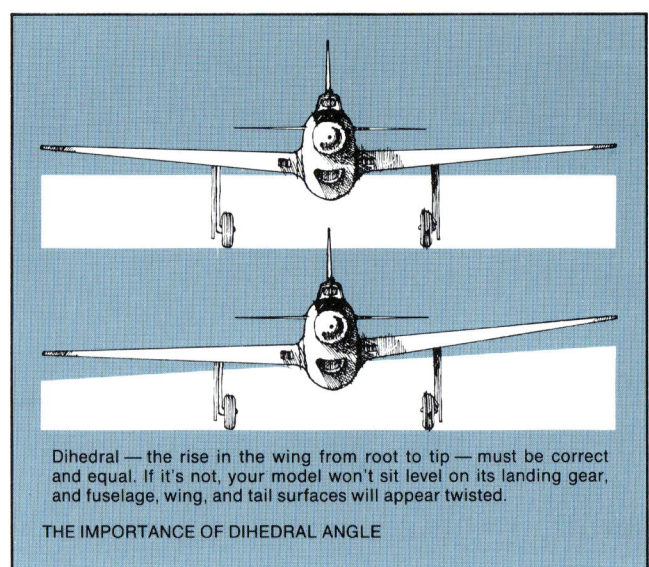

Dihedral — the rise in the wing from root to tip — must be correct and equal. If it's not, your model won't sit level on its landing gear, and fuselage, wing, and tail surfaces will appear twisted.

THE IMPORTANCE OF DIHEDRAL ANGLE

(Left) Check the dihedral angles by holding the wings tightly against the fuselage wing roots and sighting down the fuselage center line from the front. (Below left) Correct the dihedral if needed by going over the wing root with a sanding block to remove burrs, mold marks, and offset joints.

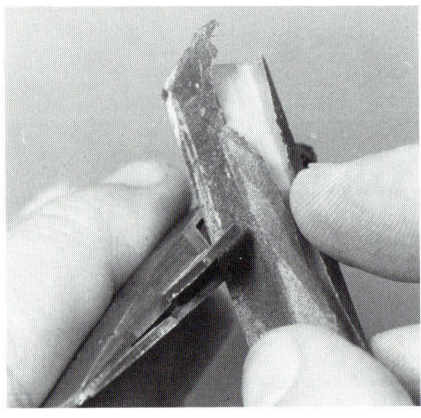

the roots to establish the correct angle and make both wings match. When they do, apply cement and hold the wings against the fuselage, constantly checking that the proper angle is maintained while the joints harden.

To ensure that the wings don't droop while the joints harden overnight, run tape supports from the wing tips to the top of the fuselage. Check that you haven't changed the angles while taping. Next day, putty gaps between wing root and fuselage or fillet as you did with the tail surfaces, sanding smooth when dry.

The dihedral on a single-piece, solid wing is molded in, and can only be changed by using a razor saw to cut partially through the wing at the appropriate spot, allowing movement up or down. This surgery is best done before cementing the wing to the fuselage. Maintain the correct dihedral by taping the wing to a board with identical blocks under each wing tip. When the altered wing has been cemented, the plastic has hardened, and the saw cut puttied, cement the wing to the fuselage, again sighting from nose to tail for correct alignment. Because of the altered dihedral you'll probably have to use filler putty on the fuselage-wing seam.

Straightening and attaching halved wings. If your kit has individual wings molded in halves, ones that butt directly against the fuselage or fillets, rub the seam edges of the wing halves on a flat piece of sandpaper, then trial fit them. Align the wing root first, since it is the thickest part of the wing and the most difficult to correct. If aligning the root means throwing the leading edge badly out of line at the tip, you may choose to make alignment of the leading edge primary, letting the chips fall where they may for the root, trailing edge, and tip.

Cement the wing root first and let it harden so you'll have a solid base to work from. Then sight down the leading edge seam, hold it straight to eliminate warps, and apply cement to a short section at a time, working from the root toward the tip. Continue to hold the parts until the seam in each cemented section remains straight on its own, then proceed to the next section.

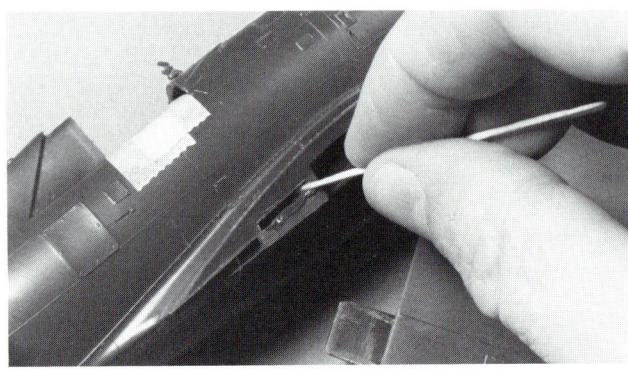

If you have tube cement, apply it in the attaching slots in the wing root with a toothpick. Use liquid cement to seal the root seams once the wings are in place.

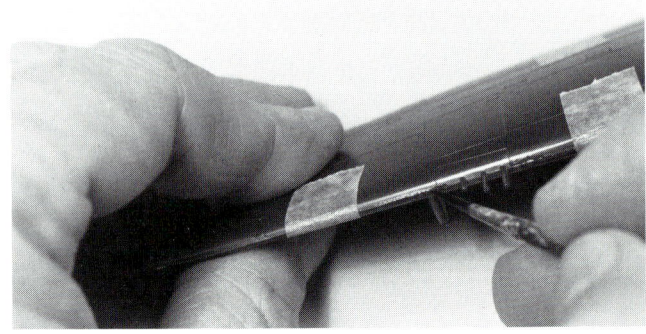

To assemble four-part wings, tape the halves together and apply cement between pieces of tape. Hold the wing straight as the cement sets to eliminate warps.

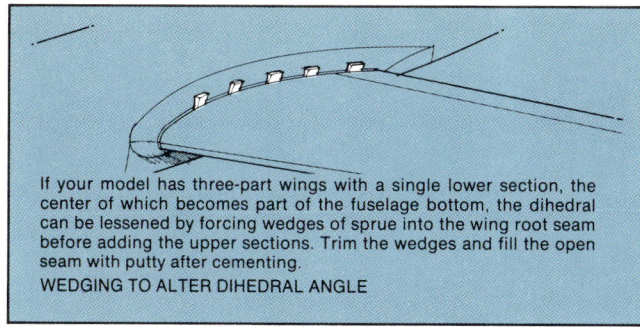

If your model has three-part wings with a single lower section, the center of which becomes part of the fuselage bottom, the dihedral can be lessened by forcing wedges of sprue into the wing root seam before adding the upper sections. Trim the wedges and fill the open seam with putty after cementing.
WEDGING TO ALTER DIHEDRAL ANGLE

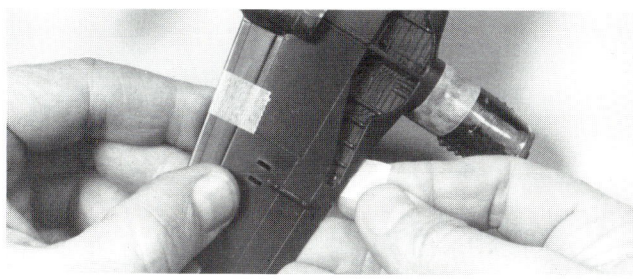
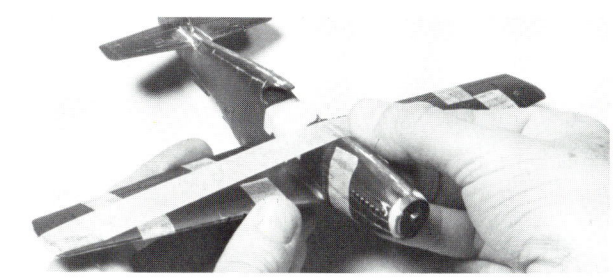

(Top) To assemble three-part wings, first trial-fit parts to the fuselage. (Above) When the top sections have been cemented in place, use tape if needed to maintain correct dihedral angles.

Check the alignment of wing top sections at the leading and trailing edges and at the root.

Work your way around the tip and down the trailing edge using the same straightening technique as on the leading edge. Then set the wing aside to dry. Assemble the second wing just like the first.

When the plastic has hardened, sand the edges for perfect alignment and smooth them to a paint-ready state. Set the dihedral angle and attach the wings to the fuselage the same way you would if the wings were molded solid.

Straightening and attaching three-part wings. If your kit is one of those designed with three-part wings — a single bottom part whose center section is a section of the fuselage, and two top parts — the assembly technique is different.

Sand the seam edges as usual, then tape the wing bottom in place, aligning it with the fuselage at front and rear, and sighting nose to tail to establish equal dihedral. Then tightly tape the wing tops to the bottom, working out warps as best you can. Don't worry about wing edge alignment; a straight seam is all you're concerned about right now.

Now sight the dihedral again, and if need be shift the lower section to equalize the angle of each wing in relation to the fuselage's vertical center line. Then cement the wing bottom to the fuselage.

Once the joint has hardened you can start worrying about aligning the edges of the top wing parts with the bottom. You may find edge alignment problems stemming from the wing root; when the root joint is aligned, the other edges are off at the tip, or when the other edges are aligned, there's a gap at the root.

If so, sanding the root of the wing top part for a better fit against the fuselage or fillet may be the answer, providing it doesn't shorten it at the tip too much. If it does, the best compromise is to opt for good leading edge alignment and fill the resulting gap at the root joint with putty later.

When you're satisfied with edge alignment, tape the wing tops to the bottom, again straightening warps. Then sight the dihedral again. If one or both wings are too low, sand the roots or fillets at an angle to correct. If one or both are too high, wedge bits of plastic shaved from the sprue trees into the root joint to force the wing down.

When your final check with wing parts taped together reveals acceptable dihedral, edge alignment, and straightness, tack cement the top parts to the wing bottom by applying tiny amounts of cement to the edge seams between the pieces of tape. Don't cement the root yet. Double-check the seams for straightness as you cement, and hand hold as needed until the joints harden. When the areas you've tack cemented are dry, remove the tape and finish cementing the edge seams.

Now — one more time — check the dihedral. If it's still okay, cement the root. If a wing is high, wedge until corrected, then cement; if a wing is low, only a razor saw cut can remove excess plastic from the root now. If you have a razor saw, make the correction. If not, matching the dihedral of the two wings by wedging the higher one down is the best you can do. Apply cement when you're ready.

Let the root joint harden overnight, sand the edges smooth, and apply putty to fill any gaps, using the tape-and-toothpick technique. Sand smooth when dry.

Now hold up the model, and there before you is a bird in flight. Your dodo has sprouted wings. You zoom it, you bank it through a couple of turns, you even consider completing it with wheels up. But no, that won't do. So you belly it in on the workbench to await painting and final assembly.

Painting this Tamiya 1/48 scale Zero required just as much care as its assembly.

4 Choosing and using paints

Showing your true colors

Now that most of the construction of your model is behind you, you probably think the hard part is over. You're only half right. Properly painting the plane requires just as much time and patience as assembling it.

Good construction and good painting go hand in hand to produce good models. The best painting can't hide poor construction, but good construction can be lost behind poor painting. You'll need the right paints and the right tools — and the right techniques to get the best from both.

Selecting model paint. We model builders are blessed — and occasionally confused — by the variety of paints developed especially for the hobby. To narrow the choices, aircraft colors are available in two basic kinds of hobby paints, the old tried-and-true oil-base enamels, and the newer water-base latexes and acrylics.

When thinned to the right consistency, oil-base enamels can be either hand brushed or airbrushed, and cleanup is with turpentine or paint thinner. The flat colors dry to the touch in a few minutes and cure completely overnight. If touch-up is required the edges of sanded areas feather easily and disappear when painted over.

On days with especially high or low humidity oil-base enamels may be balky about coming out of an airbrush, particularly when you're painting fine lines or dots. Flat enamels dry with a slight grain, and decals won't stick to them unless the painted surface is first given a coat of clear gloss.

Latex paints can also be hand brushed or airbrushed, but they seem to have been developed primarily with hand brushing in mind. They can be applied right from the bottle — no thinning — with a brush or plastic foam pad. Latex shows no brush marks or overlaps and dries perfectly flat and grainless — so smooth, in fact, that decals can be applied without adding a gloss coat. Brushes can be cleaned up with water, but the cleanup must be done immediately, while the paint is still wet.

Latex can be airbrushed on large areas with only slight thinning, and with the same flat, grainless result produced by hand brushing. But because latex must be blasted on wet and relatively thick, the finish picks up lint from the air. When thinned sufficiently with either water or alcohol to spray like oils, latex loses its normally good bonding ability.

Latex requires 24 to 48 hours of drying time, but even thin sanded edges don't feather well when touch-up is called for; the edges remain visible under the new paint. To hide touched-up areas the paint must be removed from a section within panel lines and that entire section repainted.

Airbrushes used for spraying latex must be cleaned immediately after use with warm soapy water, because latex bonds quickly and almost permanently to metal. In fact, when airbrushing large areas latex may build up so heavily on the airbrush tip that you'll have to stop and clean the tip before completing the application.

Acrylics offer the best of both worlds. They can be hand brushed out of the bottle like latex or, when thinned, airbrushed like enamel. Acrylics dry to the touch in a few minutes, bond well to plastic or other paint, and are grainless — decals can be applied with-

The sheer numbers of paint brands and variety of colors offered specifically for aircraft modeling almost boggle the imagination. Both oil-base and water-base paints can be either hand brushed or, with proper thinning, airbrushed.

out a gloss coat. Acrylics are unaffected by high or low humidity when sprayed, and allow extremely fine line painting with never a balk. Edges feather beautifully when sanded. Airbrushes and brushes clean up with water, even faster with rubbing alcohol.

Each type of paint has its own thinner, and while substitutions can be made in some cases, you'd be wise to use what the manufacturer recommends while you're learning to paint.

You'll have no trouble finding paint for your Thunderbolt, Mustang, or Zero. All major U. S. and Japanese colors used during World War Two are available in oil-base, latex, and acrylic paints. You'll need only two main colors for these three aircraft: one for the top and another for the bottom. In addition, you'll need black for the propeller blades, yellow for the tips, and silver for the landing gear. There may be more; check your kit's instruction sheet.

If you choose oil-base paints, you'll also need a clear gloss and a clear flat for applying decals later on.

To brush or not to brush? Perhaps you bought paint after reading the chapter on tools, and decided then how you'd apply it. If not, you are now at that decision point. The method of application you choose will influence the type of paint you buy.

Hand painting with brushes is relatively inexpensive, but that's the only advantage, and there are many disadvantages. Hand brushing opens up limitless opportunities for hairs, lint, and dust to get in the paint, not to mention brush marks, thin spots, puddles, runs, and sags. All of these can be overcome, of course, in time and with practice.

There are some limitations in paint schemes that can't be overcome, however. Hand brushing can only deliver sharp demarcation lines between colors, and it's impossible to reproduce mottle and feather-edge camouflage schemes.

Aerosol cans. If hand brushing suddenly doesn't sound so good to you but an airbrush still sounds too expensive, there's a half-step you might consider.

Aerosol cans offer a relatively inexpensive — but primitive — way to spray paint. The aerosol spray eliminates brush marks, and by using masks or mats you can achieve acceptably soft demarcation lines between colors. Each aerosol unit is self-contained, with paint and propellant in the same can, so there's no thinning or mixing (other than shaking).

That's about the extent of the advantages, however. The color selection is small; the spray pattern is wide and nonadjustable, which wastes a lot of paint; and the power is always on full force when you press the button.

If you'd like to try painting with an aerosol can, go outdoors or to the garage — without the car in it — or to the basement where overspray won't hurt anything. Practice on a large piece of cardboard to develop a feel for proper distance from the can to the model and the speed with which to make each pass. Spraying too close to the model causes runs; spraying too far away makes flat paint dry with a rough, pebble finish. The ideal is to move the spray pattern across the model at a speed and distance which will lay on a coat of paint that looks damp, neither shiny wet nor dull dry.

If you get good enough (and brave enough) to try aerosol painting on a model, start the spray to one side of the model and finish on the other side to prevent spots and splatters; don't stop in the middle, then start again. Spray in overlapping strokes until the model

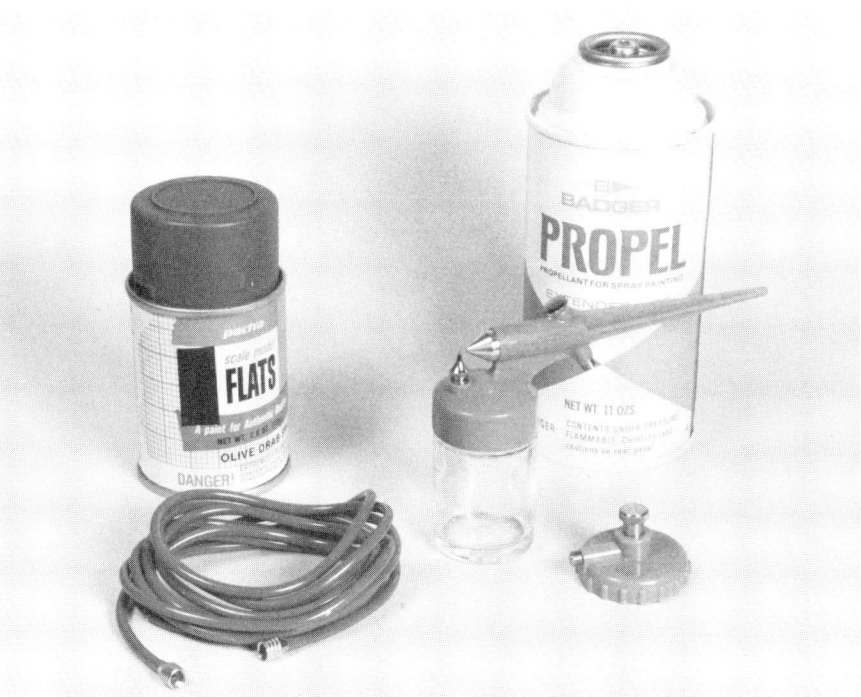

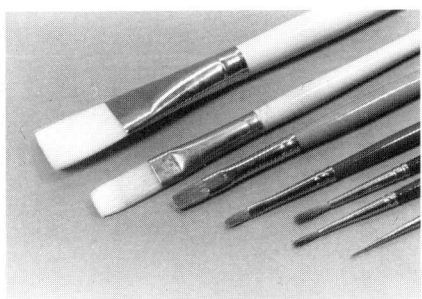

(Above) Among the inexpensive alternatives to hand brushing are aerosol spray cans and nonadjustable airbrushes with canned propellant. (Right) You'll need artist's brushes for painting small parts, but (other than cost) they offer few advantages for painting large areas.

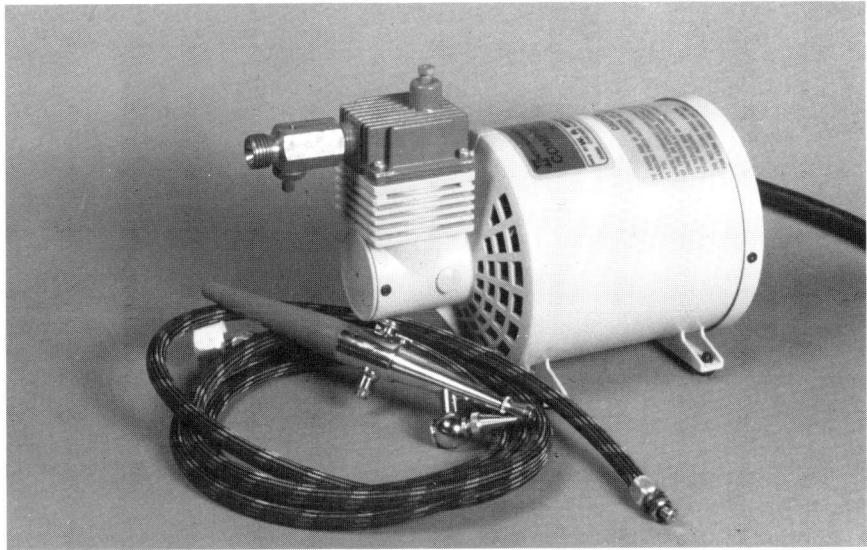

Two lifetime modeling investments that will pay for themselves many times over: an adjustable, single-action airbrush, and an air compressor to supply it.

(Left) Before painting, plug all openings in your model with wads of tissue to keep out overspray. **(Right)** Large openings such as cockpits may need tape around the edges as well as tissue in the center. A pencil or dowel serves as a handle for painting.

is covered. Let the paint dry overnight before continuing.

Clean the nozzle by holding the can upside down and pressing the button. This way only propellant comes out, quickly blowing the paint out of the nozzle. Once clear, pull the nozzle off and store it in paint thinner until the next use. Store the can on its side.

The case for airbrushing. Most serious modelers paint with airbrushes because of the variety of paints and colors available, the ability to control the spray pattern and volume of paint, and the professional appearance of the finished model.

Airbrushing doesn't have to be expensive. A simple, nonadjustable airbrush and a can of propellant cost no more than four top-quality brushes. An adjustable, single-action airbrush outfit with propellant costs only two to three times that much.

Even a nonadjustable airbrush eliminates brush marks and hairs and, when paint is not applied too heavily, eliminates most lint problems. The disadvantage of the nonadjustable airbrush is that it sprays a fairly wide pattern, which is good for covering large areas but not for fine mottle color schemes and feather-edge painting.

For only a few dollars more an adjustable, single-action airbrush — one with a tip that turns to adjust the size of the spray pattern and a button to push for air — will meet the needs of even the most experienced modeler, and can be considered a lifetime investment. Such airbrushes usually have replaceable tips, so if your interest in aircraft modeling grows, you can purchase fine and large tips to go with the medium one that comes with the airbrush.

Canned propellant is an inexpensive power source for your first attempt at airbrushing, and if you paint only a few models a year it remains inexpensive. If you paint more than that, however, you'll want to add a compressor

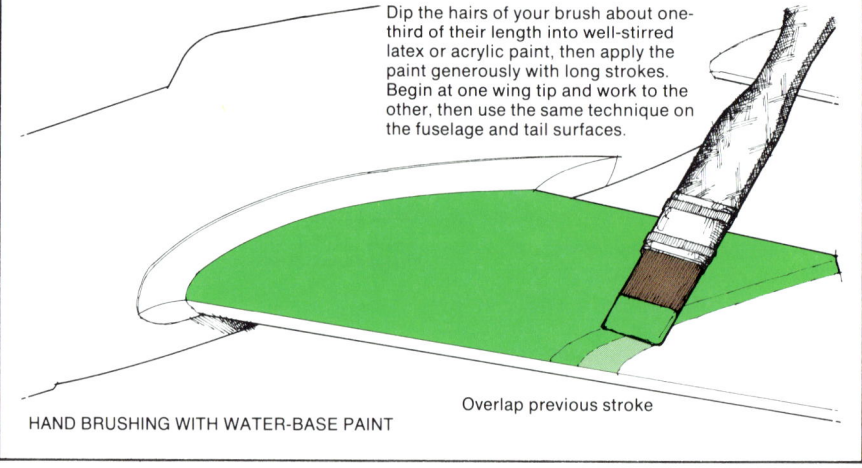

Dip the hairs of your brush about one-third of their length into well-stirred latex or acrylic paint, then apply the paint generously with long strokes. Begin at one wing tip and work to the other, then use the same technique on the fuselage and tail surfaces.

HAND BRUSHING WITH WATER-BASE PAINT — Overlap previous stroke

to your list of lifetime modeling investments — the cost of lots of propellant cans soon equals the cost of a compressor.

Your decision to paint with either aerosol cans or an airbrush may be influenced by whether you have a suitable place to use them. Spray painting requires a location with good ventilation — outdoors on a dry, windless day is okay, but a garage or basement offers all-weather convenience. Even the kitchen table or your hobby workbench may work for small jobs if you spread newspapers around to catch spills and contain the overspray with a large cardboard box.

If your choice is brushes, so be it. You'll need small brushes for painting interior details anyway, so add larger brushes to your list for exterior painting. With this decision made, you'll probably opt for latex or acrylic paints, since they lend themselves to brush painting.

If you decide to purchase an airbrush you're on your way to virtually unlimited capabilities in model aircraft color schemes. You're also more likely to achieve results similar to those in this book — all of the models you see here were painted with an airbrush, using either oil-base or acrylic paints.

Getting the model ready for paint. With all the decisions made and paint and painting equipment bought, you probably think you're ready to paint. Well almost. You're ready but your model isn't.

Plug all openings — air and oil cooler scoops, landing gear mounting sockets, and so on — with wads of facial tissue. Stuff the cowling of your Zero or Thunderbolt — if it's molded on the fuselage — with tissue, too, to protect the engine and inside of the cowling. Don't let stray bits of tissue stick out where they can flap around and become stuck in the paint later on.

Put masking tape around the inside of the cockpit opening, then either cover the top hole with more tape or stuff tissue inside to protect the cockpit interior.

Whether you plan to paint with brush or airbrush, be sure you have a way to hold the model before you start. Holding the fuselage near the cockpit may be good enough while you paint the bottom, but there are few appendages on the bottom to grasp while you work on the top. Depending on your

(Left) Before painting color coats, check the seams for imperfections by priming with light gray. (Above) Sand the primed seams, wash the model, and it's ready for finish coats.

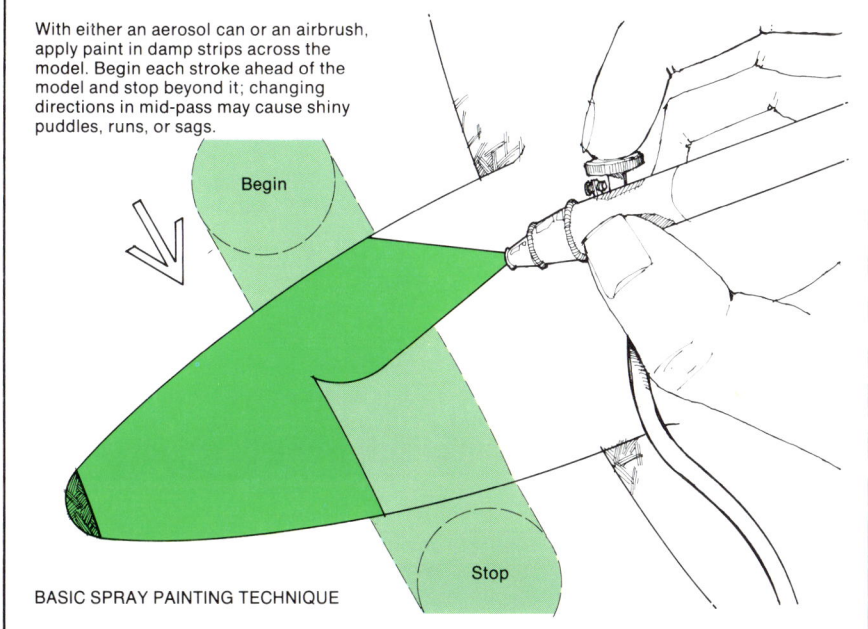

With either an aerosol can or an airbrush, apply paint in damp strips across the model. Begin each stroke ahead of the model and stop beyond it; changing directions in mid-pass may cause shiny puddles, runs, or sags.

BASIC SPRAY PAINTING TECHNIQUE

kit, you may be able to make a handle by sticking a pencil or piece of dowel or wire through a hole in the nose — but don't push it so far that you damage the cockpit. Tape the handle so the model doesn't move around.

You can make a support rack for painting by plugging three 6" pieces of coat hanger wire into holes drilled in a board in the approximate positions of the main landing gear and tail wheel. Grind a blunt point on the end of each wire, then bend the wires so each fits into one of the sockets for the main gear and tail wheel. Such a rack will hold the model even if it is tipped as much as 30 degrees.

Revealing the flaws. Now you're ready to test the quality of your construction. Brush or spray a light coat of the gray paint you chose for the model's underside on all of your carefully sanded seams. Imperfections — sanding marks, unfilled seams, putty pits — will leap out at you. When the paint is dry, remedy the problems and paint again. Keep at it until you get it right, then sand all the painted areas lightly with 600 paper and water, feathering the edges of the paint onto the plastic.

Now head for the sink once more to wash your model. Use water and a little detergent, but work carefully. Don't get water in your plugged openings where it would ruin the masking, and don't allow it inside the model where it would leak out during painting and spoil the finish. Dip an old, soft toothbrush into the water and work on one small area at a time, merely moistening the surface. Rinse the same way, then dry the model with a lintless paper dish cloth.

Brush painting techniques. Now, at last, you're ready for some serious painting. Since dark colors cover light ones easily, but not vice versa, paint the bottom of the model first. When it's dry, paint the top.

If you're hand brushing with latex or acrylic, start by stirring the paint thoroughly, especially acrylics, then dip the hairs of your brush about a third of their length into the paint. Brush the paint generously onto the model with long overlapping strokes, beginning at one wing tip and working to the other, covering the fuselage and tail surfaces in between.

Brush only in one direction; don't scrub back and forth. If bubbles appear in latex, don't worry; they'll go away on their own without leaving a mark. Don't let the paint puddle in low places. While you can go back and cover missed spots while the paint is still shiny wet, don't try to do so if the paint has started to dry. Instead, wait until the first coat is thoroughly dry, then apply a second coat.

When the first coat of bottom color is complete, set the model aside to dry until tomorrow. Don't test it; don't touch it — just wait until tomorrow. Full-size fingerprints have ruined more small-scale paint jobs than any other form of disaster.

After the paint dries overnight, sand out hairs and lint before applying a second coat if needed. If it's not needed, don't do it; if the first coat covered nicely, there's no need to build up extra layers of paint.

If you're brush painting with oil-base paint, the techniques for application are much the same as for latex and acrylic. Oil and pigment separate in the containers, and a lot of stirring is required. In most cases the paint must be thinned.

Pour some stirred paint into another container, add a small amount of thinner, and stir well. Test the consistency by brushing some of the paint on a piece of cardboard or scrap, then add more thinner if needed. Paint that's just right will flow out of the brush like ink and cover in one coat without leaving brush marks; paint that's too thick will not cover well, will leave brush marks, and will gum up the brush;

Since wheel well doors are the same color as the undersides of the model, stick them to a board and paint them at the same time as the bottom of the plane.

paint that's too thin will flow like water and won't cover well.

Cleaning brushes. No matter what type of paint you use, clean the brush as soon as you've finished painting. Water will take out latex and acrylic; turpentine or thinner will take out oils. Be gentle with the hairs — don't scrub or pull on them. Dip the brush into the cleaning solvent, then stroke it on a paper towel or rag as though you're painting it. Keep dipping and painting until you're brushing only clear solvent, then form the point into the right shape and store the brush with its point up in a container where nothing can touch or bend the hairs.

Basic airbrushing techniques. Oil-base paints and acrylics have to be thinned more for airbrushing than for brush painting. A ratio of one part paint to one part thinner works well for most airbrushes.

After you've stirred and thinned the paint, test the consistency by spraying a piece of cardboard. If the paint is too thick the spray will be coarse and perhaps lumpy, and you'll have to add more thinner. If too thin, the spray will be watery and the paint will tend to run and won't cover well. When you have a fine, damp spray that covers in a couple of passes you're ready to paint the model.

You'll have a lot more control, but paint application with an airbrush is about the same as with aerosol cans. Hold the airbrush 6″ to 9″ from the model and start the spray to one side of the model, keeping it going until the spray pattern has passed to the other side. This way the little drops of paint that build up on the tip of the airbrush at the end of each pass won't spatter on the plane.

Move the spray pattern across the model at a speed that lays a damp strip across the model, neither shiny wet nor dull dry. To prevent missed or thin spots, make each pass overlap the previous one. Don't stop or reverse directions in mid pass with the spray on; you'll create a puddle that will take a while to dry, will probably be shinier than the rest of the paint, and may even run or sag.

When the entire surface has been sprayed give the paint a few minutes to dry. Then spray on a second coat just as you did the first, but this time turn the model 90 degrees, so each pass is at right angles to the first ones. This should eliminate thin spots in the paint coat.

Now set the model aside and let the paint dry overnight to maximum hardness before touching, masking, or painting the dark upper surfaces. While you still have the gray paint in the airbrush, stick the wheel well covers to a board with double-sided tape and paint

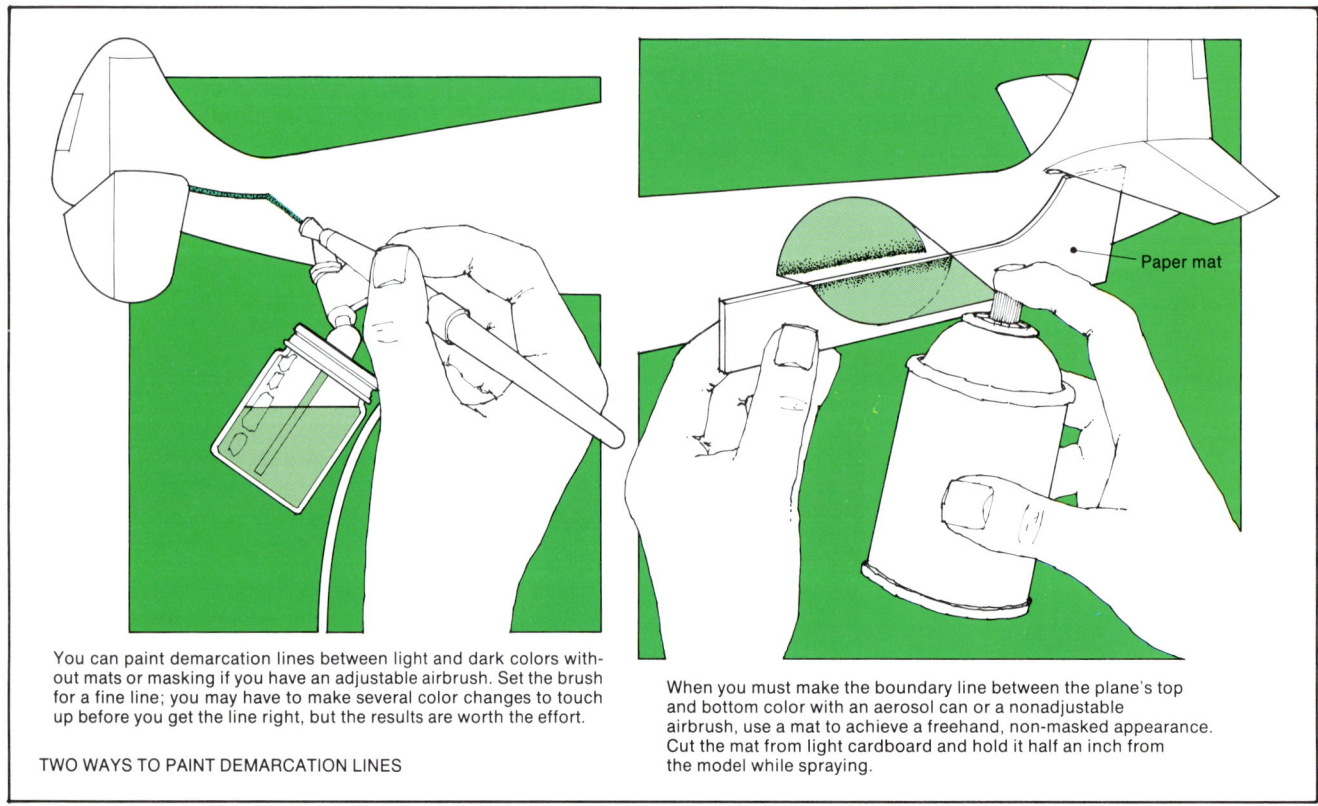

You can paint demarcation lines between light and dark colors without mats or masking if you have an adjustable airbrush. Set the brush for a fine line; you may have to make several color changes to touch up before you get the line right, but the results are worth the effort.

TWO WAYS TO PAINT DEMARCATION LINES

When you must make the boundary line between the plane's top and bottom color with an aerosol can or a nonadjustable airbrush, use a mat to achieve a freehand, non-masked appearance. Cut the mat from light cardboard and hold it half an inch from the model while spraying.

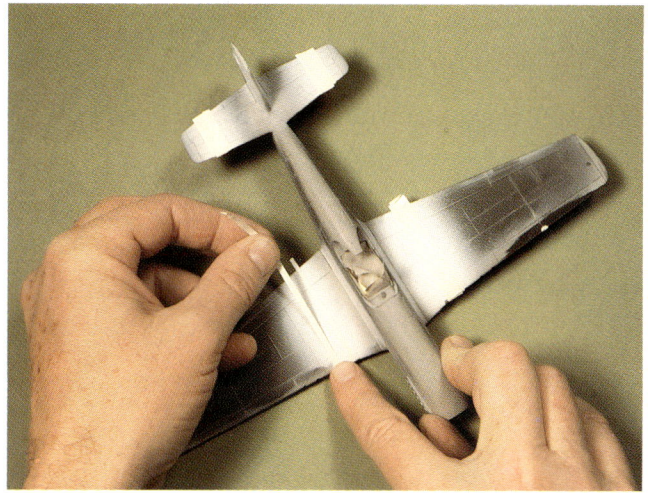

Often it's best to paint white identification stripes before the dark upper colors are applied, then mask the stripes with tape (above). Once the demarcation lines between the top and bottom colors are painted on, the remaining portions are coated with broad strokes of the airbrush (right). (Above right) With masking tape removed, this 1/48 scale Mustang begins to look like a real airplane.

them, too, since they're the same color as the bottom of the model.

Clean the airbrush by first wiping out the paint cup or bottle, then spraying solvent (turpentine or thinner for oil-base paint, water or rubbing alcohol for acrylic) through it to flush the passages. Dismantling the airbrush for cleaning is rarely necessary if it's thoroughly flushed after each use.

Applying the top color. Once the bottom color has dried, you can paint the top surfaces. It won't be as easy, however. You must be a little neater because you have a demarcation line between the colors to worry about. Here, if you're brush painting, you actually have fewer worries. You have no choice but to brush on the top color and take what you get — a hard, brushed line — for the boundary.

Airbrushing is a different story. On the real plane the demarcation line between the light underside color and the dark upper one was formed by the edge of a paint gun's spray pattern, so on the model the line should appear feathered. You can simulate this with a nonadjustable airbrush by cutting thin cardboard into a mat of the proper shape and holding it a slight distance from the side of the model while you spray. Practice by spraying against a large piece of cardboard, varying the distance until the feathered edge looks right.

With an adjustable airbrush you should be able to paint a feathered edge without the cardboard mask. Practice until you can lay a fine line on a piece of cardboard before you try it on the model.

Don't be discouraged if even after practicing your feathered edge doesn't come out quite right the first time. If it needs more dark color, spray it on. If there's too much, clean the airbrush, go back to the light color again, and touch up. Even experienced modelers may change colors several times before they get it right.

Once you're satisfied with the color boundary lines, paint the rest of the upper surfaces, using the same technique you used for the lower ones. Then clean the brush or airbrush.

Painting the canopy. The painted portions of the canopy should be taken care of at the same time the upper surfaces are painted, since the paint is mixed and ready.

With a steady hand or a convenient hand rest you may be able to do a creditable job of painting the frame lines between the clear portions of the canopy with a brush. If you're not that steady, some sort of liquid mask may be your answer. Liquid mask is a rubber-cement-like preparation that can be brushed on the clear parts, allowed to dry, trimmed along the paint lines for straightness, and peeled off the frame areas. After the frames are painted the rest of the mask is peeled away.

Masking tape and brush painting don't work well together anywhere, and canopies are no exception. Part of the large amount of paint that the

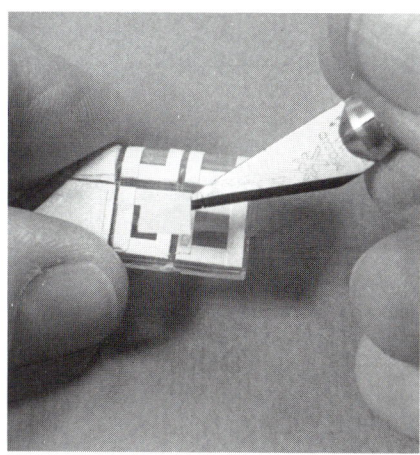

Mask canopy frame outlines with thin strips of tape, then fill in the centers with larger pieces.

The crisp color demarcation line between the upper and lower colors on this 1/72 scale Thunderbolt was masked, not sprayed. Also note the trim stripes on the tail surfaces. (Model and photo by Bob Angel.)

brush applies may run under the tape, creating problems in cleaning off the clear areas later. The relatively large volume of paint, when dry, often leaves a thick, rough edge when the tape is removed.

Masking is the only way to airbrush clear parts. Liquid mask works well here, as does masking tape. A single piece of tape can be applied to overlap a section, then the edges trimmed to fit with a hobby knife. Or, if the frame edges are hard to find when covered with tape, each clear section can be outlined with tiny strips of tape and the centers filled in with larger pieces trimmed to fit. Mask the interior of the canopy completely to keep out overspray.

When using either painting method, be sure to paint the edges of the canopy. Some edges may be exposed and visible when the canopy is glued in place, especially the lower edges. But even if not exposed, the edges will be visible when you look down through the plastic, and they'll have a silvery, unreal look to them. Painting hides this.

Painting trim. Once the final coat of paint has dried you're ready to paint trim. Many Mustangs and Thunderbolts had colored noses and tails; Zeros had black cowlings. If you're hand brushing, simply apply the trim color to the proper areas. If airbrushing, you must mask off the areas to be painted. At the demarcation line use a thin strip of tape which will conform easily to compound curves, overlap the thin strip with a wider piece, then tape on pieces of tissue to cover the rest of the model to keep off overspray.

Because of the difficulty in covering dark colors with light, it's best to spray white identification stripes on the model before you paint the main camouflage colors, then mask over the white. You can get the white to cover the darker colors, but the thickness of the paint will be noticeable.

Touching up and solving problems. So now you've successfully painted your model — or maybe it's only a qualified success. If so, the problems probably include runs or sags, paint that dried rough and sandpapery, or too much overspray from the upper surfaces on the lower.

None of these problems are cause for throwing away your model. Often the success of a good model depends on how well the boo-boos are hidden. A good paint job, even by the pros, is seldom achieved without some touching up.

Runs and sags can be sanded away when the paint is thoroughly dry, as can the sandpaper effect, and the areas repainted. The answer to runs and sags is not to put on too much paint in one coat. Many light coats are better than a single heavy one. The sand-finish problem is often caused by holding the airbrush too far from the model, which allows the paint to dry before it gets there, or it can be caused by turbulence in a fillet, which creates overspray that dries in the air, then settles on the still-wet paint in the fillet. Generally this can be taken care of by spraying light coats of paint into the fillet at an angle from front to back, which should blow the overspray away.

If traces of one color are oversprayed on another they can sometimes be removed by using toothpaste or tooth polish (not a gel) as an extra-fine rubbing compound. Barely moisten a cloth or cotton swab with water, dab on a tiny amount of toothpaste, and rub gently on the offending overspray. If the paint is not too heavy it should come off easily. An unfortunate side effect is that the rubbing will make your dull military finish slightly shiny, and you'll have to make it dull again with a coat of clear flat finish.

A more drastic way to eliminate overspray is to sand lightly with wet 600 sandpaper, trying not to go through the paint underneath. Here again you'll need a coat of clear flat to restore the paint's normal dull appearance. The way to deal with heavy overspray is to paint over it with the proper color. Of course, this gives rise to the opportunity for more overspray on the opposite colored surface unless a mat is used to screen it.

If paint pulls off along with the masking tape after trim painting the most likely cause is that the model was not washed thoroughly before painting. Sand the paint around the bare spot to feather the edges, then wash and repaint the area.

You probably thought painting was easy. Now you find that it calls for as much skill and patience — maybe even more — as construction. But by doing a good job on each you now have a model that, even without landing gear, propeller, and canopy, looks more and more like a miniature version of the real thing.

Combining painted-on stripes and markings applied with decals brings this Mustang to life.

5 Applying decal markings

Establishing an identity

Your model looks rather sleek now with its two-tone paint job, but it's still somewhat bland without any distinguishing marks. This is the time to add some, while there are no propellers, antenna masts, landing gear, and wheel well doors to get in the way.

Applying a gloss coat. If you used oil-base paint on your model, there's no avoiding the need to coat the model with clear gloss to make it smooth and shiny. The surface of even the best flat oil-base paint is rough enough that decals simply lie across the tops of the bumps. The decals won't adhere well, and the tiny pockets of air trapped underneath give the clear areas a silvery look. The markings won't have the realistic, painted-on look of properly applied decals.

To counteract this, fill the valleys between the little bumps by brushing or spraying clear gloss over the entire model until it has a varnished look. Let the finish dry overnight, then wet sand out any bits of lint caught in it.

If you painted your model with latex or acrylic paint there's no need for the gloss coat. These paints dry to a smooth finish that decals stick to quite well. When your final coat — gloss, latex, or acrylic — is dry, you're ready to apply the markings.

Trimming and applying decals. Decals are made by applying colored lacquers to a thin, clear, film base glued to a heavy, blotter-like backing paper. The clear film usually extends beyond the lacquer, and will show up as an un-

Before decals can be applied to flat camouflage colors a clear gloss coat must be added. An airbrush is the best way to do this.

When cutting individual decal markings from the sheet cut as close as possible to the painted design; leave no border.

25

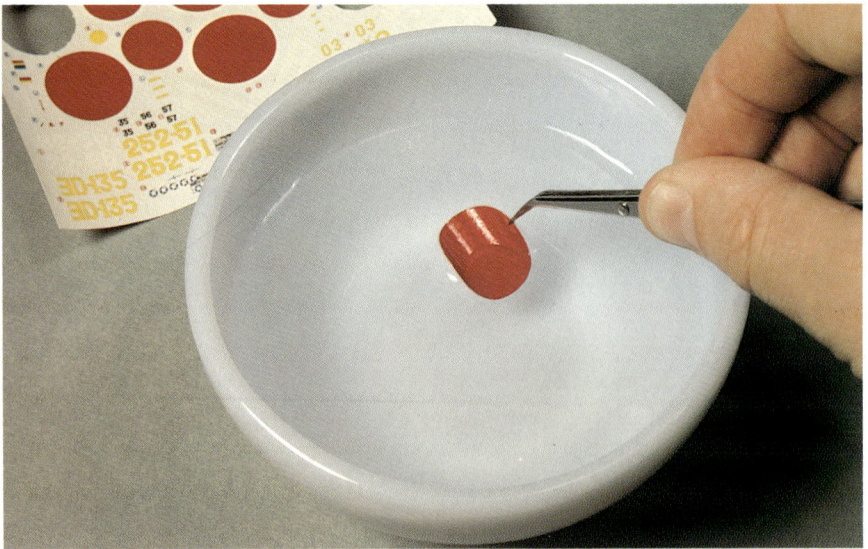

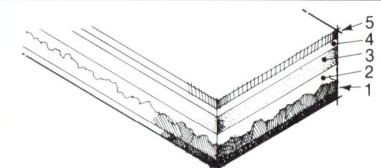

This exaggerated wing cross section shows the five layers of a decal that looks painted on. Flat camouflage paint (1) has a rough surface that decals will not adhere to, so apply clear gloss (2) to provide a smooth surface to which they can adhere. After applying the decal (3), another coat of clear gloss (4) is added to give the markings the same overall sheen as the rest of the model. A final goat of clear flat finish (5) provides a realistic military matte look.
APPLYING DECALS

(Above) Place one marking at a time in warm water for ten seconds, then let the moisture soak through for at least half a minute to loosen the decal from its backing. (Below) Use a toothpick to slide the decal off the backing onto a puddle of water on the model.

Applying a setting agent will wrinkle the decal at first, but as it dries the marking will flatten out again and conform to the aircraft surface.

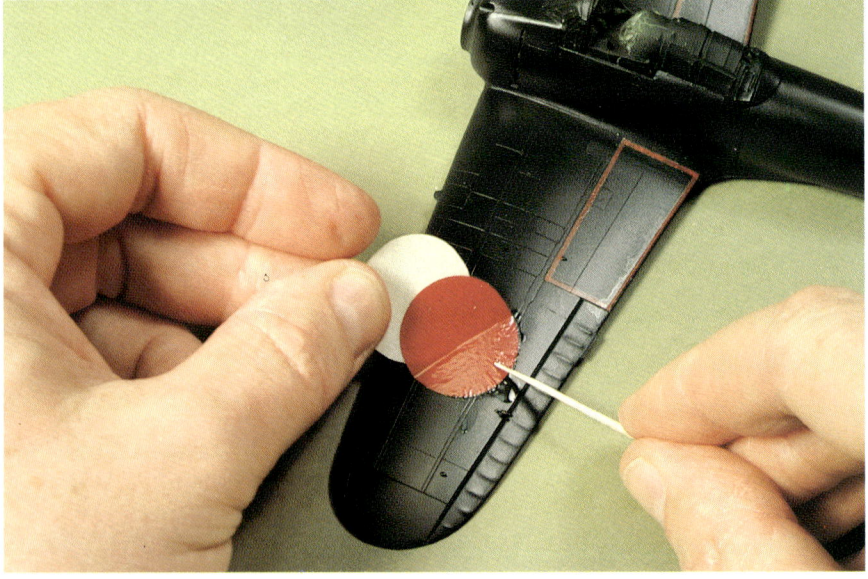

wanted (and unrealistic) border if not trimmed away. When you cut each marking from the decal sheet supplied with the kit, trim as close as you can to the edge of the paint.

Because their outlines are simple, national markings are generally easy to trim. Large unit markings — usually letters and numbers — are harder to trim, and complex unit badges, individual aircraft names, and tail codes are next to impossible.

Until you have experience in trim-

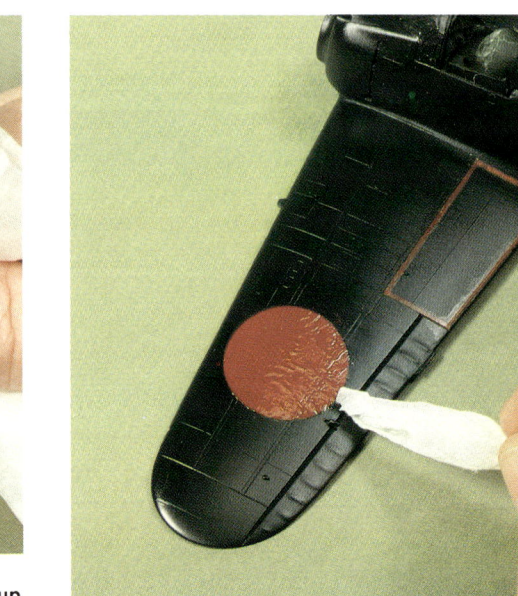

(Right) Drain away excess water from the decal by soaking it up with the corner of a tissue, then (above) gently roll out trapped air bubbles with a tissue-wrapped finger.

(Above) When the decals have dried, wash the model to remove excess decal adhesive and water stains, dry it, then give it a coat of clear gloss to blend the decal markings with the painted surface. (Right) When the clear gloss has dried, apply a coat of clear flat to restore the military matte finish.

ming and decaling, trim only to the outside edge of each decal. The reason is that when wet, decals are extremely fragile, and any odd-shaped appendages left after trimming can be easily torn off. The severed parts can be placed on the model and moved back together, and when dry the marking will look like a single piece again. But keeping small parts from being lost and moving them around without flip-flopping or folding over on themselves can be a nightmarish experience.

Cut only one marking at a time from the backing sheet. Dip it in warm water for 10 seconds, then lay it on a tissue for 30 seconds while the water soaks through and loosens the layer of glue that holds the film to the paper backing. Keep in mind that this glue also sticks the decal to the model, and soaking the decal until it floats free of the backing can dilute the glue so much that the marking may not adhere well.

After half a minute, gently test the decal to see if it has soaked loose from the backing. If the film slides easily, it's ready to apply. If not, don't force it; it can be easily torn. Wait a few more seconds and try again. It's rare, but occasionally a second dip in the warm water may be required.

Brush a few drops of warm, clear water on the model where the marking is to go. This little puddle will allow you to float the decal into position. Slide the decal partway off its backing, then grasp the backing paper with your fingers or tweezers. Now slide the decal off the backing and onto the puddle, moving it with the blunt end of a toothpick. Don't use anything sharp; you'll tear the film or punch a hole in it.

Move the marking into perfect alignment and soak away the excess water from the decal and puddle by gently touching them with the corner of a tissue. Check alignment a final time, correct it if necessary, then press the decal onto the model with a tissue.

If air bubbles are trapped under the decal film, work them toward the edge with a rolling motion of a tissue-wrapped finger. Don't try to push bubbles out; you may tear the decal.

Decal setting agents. Where markings must be applied over raised areas such as rivets, seam lines, and inspection plates, or depressed areas such as aileron or rudder joints, you may need to soften the decal with something stronger than water to make it conform to the surface irregularities. Your hobby dealer has decal setting agents for this purpose. These are simply brushed on the decal and allowed to stand until they evaporate.

When a setting agent is applied to a decal on a clear gloss finish, the decal will wrinkle badly, but will flatten out again on its own and become perfectly smooth.

On latex or acrylic paints the decal will also wrinkle if you let it, but it won't flatten out again. The technique here is to dab on a small amount of setting agent in the area to be softened, and after a few seconds press down on the decal with a tissue, which also blots away the excess moisture. Keep up this procedure until the decal softens and conforms. When all decals have been applied, set the model aside to dry overnight.

Touching up. In the light of a new day you may find that despite your best efforts there are small bubbles or wrinkles under a few markings. These can usually be eliminated by pricking the decal film with a pin or slicing through it with your hobby knife, which will allow the setting agent you dab on to get underneath the film. Eventually, by alternately dabbing setting agent and pressing down with a tissue, you should be able to make the decal conform.

If you sliced a decal to make it conform to a deep depression such as an aileron hinge line, you may end up with a gap in the marking. This gap can be touched up with the proper paint color or patched with a section cut from an unused decal.

When the repair work is dry, return to the sink and wash the model again with a mild detergent and water solution to remove the excess decal glue from the finish and markings. Rinse the model with clear water and dry.

If your model is gloss coated, give it another coat of gloss over everything, decals and all. This will give the markings and the paint the same shiny finish. When the gloss coat is dry, apply a coat of clear flat, and both decals and paint will take on the same degree of dullness. More than one coat of flat may be needed for a completely flat finish. Spray on the flat lightly, so that it looks dull as it goes on, not the shiny wet look you use for colors. If you put clear flat on wet and shiny, it may dry shiny.

If you applied your decals directly to a latex or acrylic finish, you probably have been left with shiny decals on a flat paint job. For a consistent flat appearance, one which will make the decals look painted on, give the entire model a coat of clear flat as a final step.

Remove mold marks from all small parts (such as the radial engine cylinder assembly shown here) before painting.

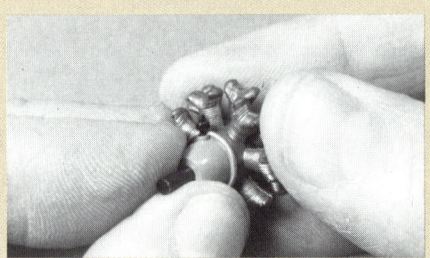

(Left) Hand brushing is the simplest way to paint the cylinders on engines molded to fire walls. (Above) When the paint has dried, remove masking and cement the engine parts together.

6 Preparing small parts for assembly

Little things mean a lot

Little things — engines, propellers, landing gear, wheels, guns, bombs — mean a lot to the final appearance of your model. You may have done the world's best construction and paint jobs on the airframe, but the effect will be lost if small parts show mold marks or are poorly shaped or poorly painted.

Generally, the techniques for preparing small parts are the same as for big ones: Sand off the mold marks, assemble, finish seams, wash and dry, and paint. The nice thing about working with small parts is that you don't have to rush; you can sandwich small-part preparation between major operations. For instance, while you're waiting for fuselage or wing seams to harden after cementing, you can work on landing gear parts and wheels. By doing so, the little pieces will be ready for final assembly about the same time the airframe is finished.

Working with engines. The only exception to this leisurely pace may be the engine. Most 1/48 scale Thunderbolt and Zero kits have cowlings molded separately from the rest of the fuselage, allowing the engine to be added any time after the interior of the cowling is painted. But some 1/72 scale kits call for the engine to be installed before the fuselage halves go together. If so, you can't wait: You must prepare the engine along with other fuselage interior parts.

On radial engines construction is usually a matter of scraping and sanding off mold marks, although some 1/48 scale engines call for a certain amount of assembly. If the gear case is molded separate from the cylinders, so much the better — it's easier to paint that way.

Together or apart, after removing mold marks paint the gear case first. Usually it's a semigloss medium gray, but check the painting instructions to be sure. Let the gear case dry overnight, then paint the cylinders: Thunderbolts are usually aluminum and Zeros are black.

Then, where required, assemble the engine parts and install the completed engine when called for by the instructions. If you have a Mustang kit with an in-line engine in it, don't bother installing the engine in your first plane, since it can't be seen. Put it in the spares box for an engine-changing diorama you'll build a few years from now.

Propellers. The edges of propeller blades are especially good at hiding mold marks — at least until they're painted — so scrape and sand them carefully, particularly down near the hub. If the instructions call for yellow tips on the blades, paint these first, as with any other light color, and when the yellow dries follow with the black that is inevitably called for.

If the hub or spinner is silver, paint it last, because most silver model paints can't be masked without pulling off part of their gloss. If your propeller has a separate spinner the painting problem is simplified; you can paint it whenever you like.

Landing gear. Landing gear struts are intricate items with a mold mark down every tiny part. In scraping and sanding these parts be careful to maintain the roundness of the oleo strut: Flat spots will show when painted. Scrape out the insides of the oleo hinges, too.

U. S. Army Air Corps planes usually had landing gear struts painted silver; those on Zeros were black. But on all

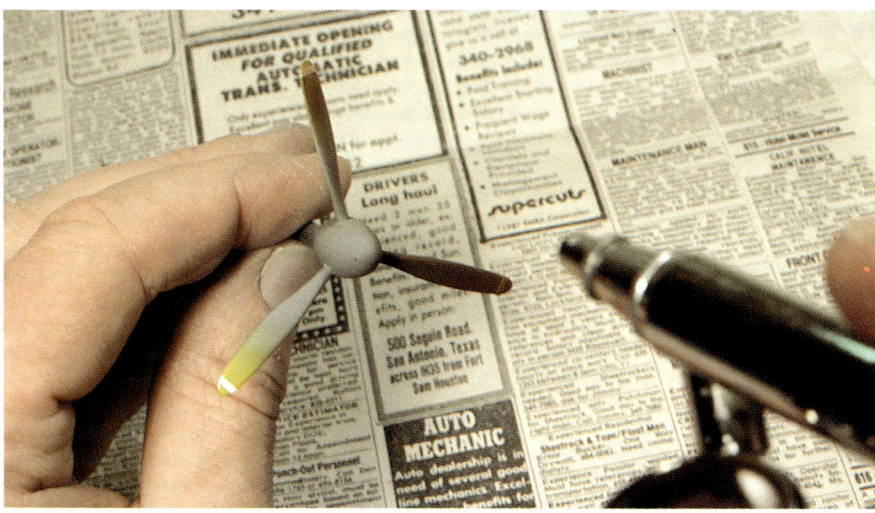

Paint the light colors (tips and stripes, usually) on propellers first, then mask them and apply the darker overall colors to the blades.

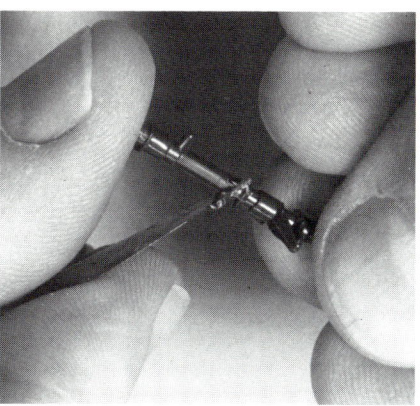

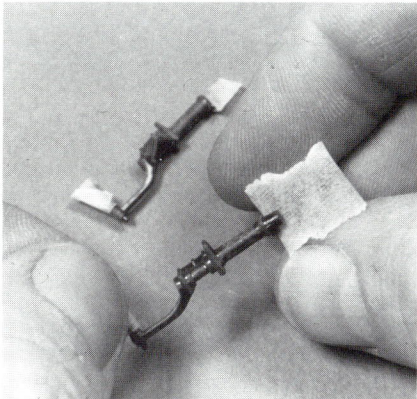

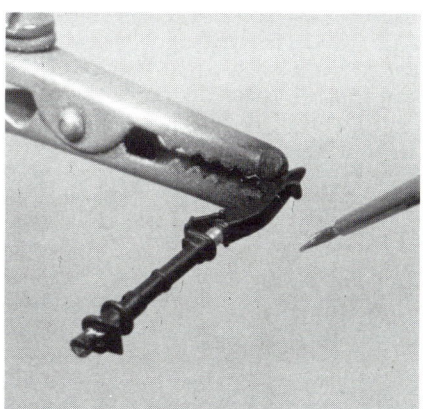

(Top) Careful scraping and sanding are required to remove mold marks yet retain the round cross section of landing gear struts. (Center) Masking areas to be cemented means you won't have to scrape away paint later. (Above) Brush silver enamel on the sliding portion of the landing gear strut to simulate chrome.

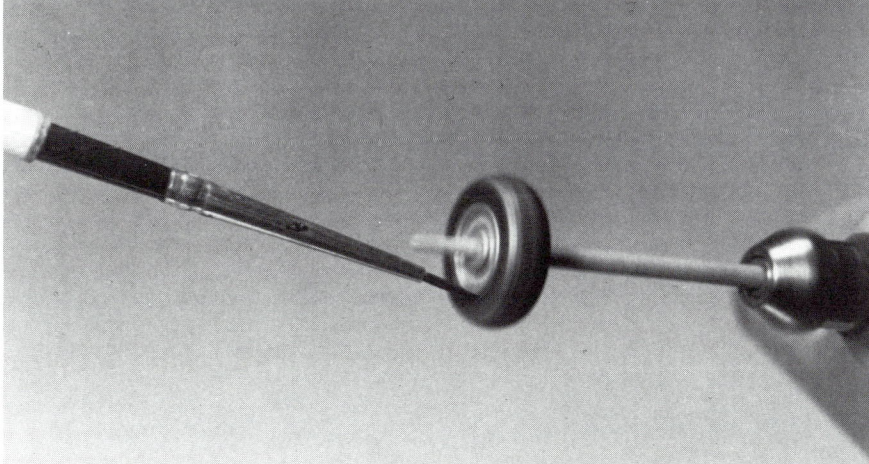

Three ways to achive a sharp demarcation line between wheel and tire. (Top) Allowing thinned paint to flow from the brush around a raised wheel rim, (above) holding a brush against a wheel and tire being spun in a drill or motor tool, and (right) airbrushing the tire while holding a cover — here a section of brass tubing — over the painted wheel.

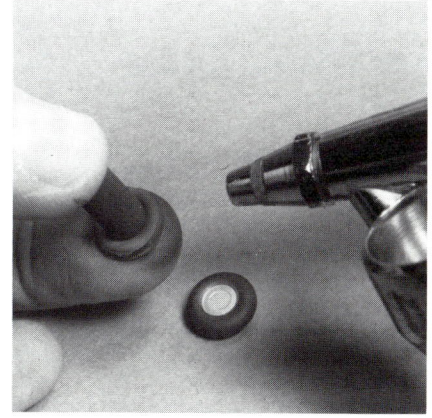

the sliding section of the oleo strut was chrome. You can simulate this by brushing the sliding section with bright silver. To make the oleo section stand out more on Thunderbolts and Mustangs paint the main portion of the strut with flat aluminum. If you airbrush the main struts, tape the axles and the portions of the struts that plug into the mounting sockets in the wings

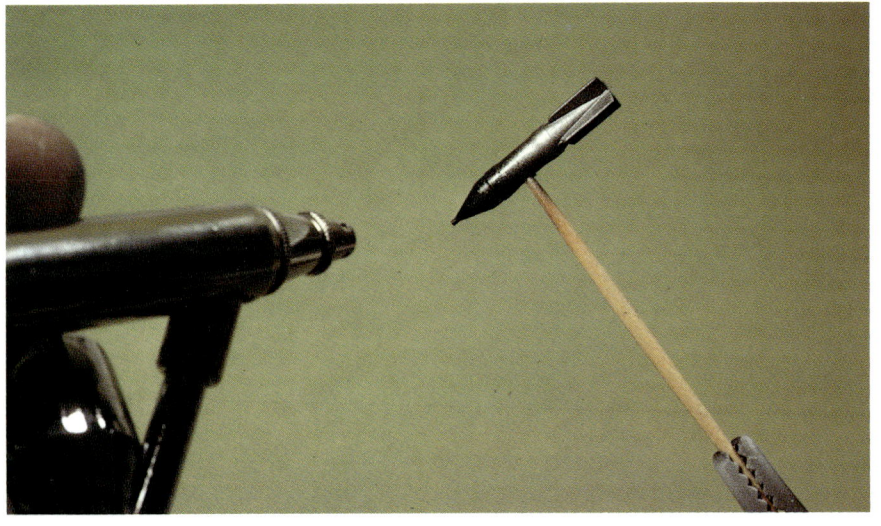
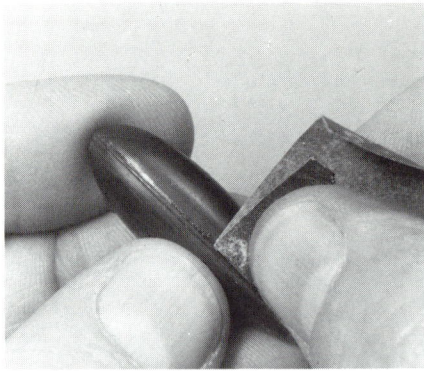

(Above) Prepare drop tanks for painting as if they were miniature fuselages. (Left) Drill holes in small objects like this bomb, then skewer them on toothpicks so you can paint all surfaces in one step.

to save having to scrape them later.

Wheels and tires. Few small touches will add more to the appearance of your finished model than perfectly circular demarcation lines between wheels and tires, and few things will detract more than wobbly ones. Lucky are those modelers whose kit provides separate wheels and tires; the demarcation line is built in. Tires can be stuck on a pencil or rolled paper cylinder and painted with abandon, wheels can be stuck to a board with double-sided tape and painted with equal ease, and the parts can be assembled when the paint is dry.

Many kits feature combined wheel-and-tire parts which are split into vertical halves. Some have instructions to put one half on the landing gear axle, spread the end of the axle with a hot knife to hold the half in place, then cement the second half to the first. Rarely as you learn model building will you want to deviate from the manufacturer's instructions, but this is one of those times. To follow these instructions is the most direct route to misaligned, poorly painted wheels you can take.

Experienced modelers cement the wheel halves together off the model, finish the seams, paint the wheels and tires, then set them aside to be added during final assembly.

Wheels and tires that are molded together, whether assembled from halves or molded as a single piece, call for all the painting skill you can muster to achieve a perfect demarcation line between wheel and tire. If you're brush painting, start by stuffing pieces of tissue into the axle sockets, painting the wheels, and letting them dry.

When it's time to paint the tires don't attempt to brush the tire color around the rims. Most wheels have a raised flange that creates a miniature dam between wheel and tire. Allow thinned paint to flow off the brush against the flange, forming its own perfect circle. If there is no flange, try impaling the wheel on a toothpick or other convenient spindle, then turn the wheel while holding the brush steady. Once the demarcation line has been painted, paint the rest of the tire.

If you're airbrushing, hold a button, washer, or any round item of the right size against the wheel and spray on the tire color.

Extra fuel tanks and bombs. The Thunderbolt, Mustang, and Zero all carried auxiliary fuel tanks on long missions, and most kits supply the tanks either as solid parts or in halves. Preparing solid drop tanks for painting is simply a matter of removing mold marks; those molded in halves should be treated like miniature fuselages. Check the instructions for the right paint colors.

In addition to its role as a fighter escort the Thunderbolt frequently served as a ground support aircraft, carrying bombs. If you decide to model this option treat each bomb as you did the drop tanks, with one additional step: Sand down the edges of the fins to disguise their over-scale thickness. If there are no appendages on the bomb to clip onto while painting, drill a small hole in the bomb body where it will be hidden when attached to the rack, then stick the end of a toothpick in it to serve as a painting handle.

Guns. Guns on Mustang models are no problem — they don't show. The gun barrels on a Thunderbolt protrude from the wings, and on the model the parts will no doubt need mold marks removed. Paint the barrels silver to simulate the T-bolt's metal protective covers.

The Zero's machine guns were hidden under the foredeck in front of the cockpit, but the cannon barrels on the late models stuck out of the wing. These will need mold mark work, no doubt, as well as painting. For a reasonably accurate gun metal color, try mixing one part silver to three parts flat black.

Antennas and pitot tubes. Your model may have other small parts that are molded separately, including radio antenna masts and pitot tubes. If so, sand, wash, and paint them as you've done the other small parts, and set them aside for final assembly — which is the next step. Exciting, isn't it?

Adding carefully prepared small parts to the carefully prepared airframe was the last step in building this Monogram 1/48 scale P-47 Thunderbolt.

7 Final assembly techniques

Getting it all together

The airframe of your model is ready and so are all the small parts. There's nothing left to do but add the little parts to the big one.

The procedure will generally go like this: For your Zero or Thunderbolt with a separate cowling, cement the engine inside the cowling, or on the front of the fuselage — wherever the instructions say.

When the engine is firmly attached, cement the cowling to the airframe. This is one of the few times when you may need to use tube cement, because you may be unable to reach inside the cowl flaps with a brush to apply liquid cement to the joint. While you may be able to puddle liquid cement on each surface and dissolve enough plastic for it to stay softened until the surfaces can be joined, a single application of tube cement will stay moist until you can join the parts.

Landing gear and wheels. When the cowling is securely mounted get ready to attach the main landing gear. Pull out the little pieces of tissue you stuffed in the wheel well sockets before painting the bottom of the plane. Didn't you do it? Then scrape out the paint with your hobby knife. Remove the tape from the tops of your landing gear struts, or scrape the paint off. Test fit the struts in their sockets to make sure they fit easily. If they don't, don't force them; scrape away plastic until they do.

If you use tube cement put a tiny amount in one socket, not on the strut, and push the strut into place. This pushes excess cement inside the socket; do it the other way and the socket scrapes the excess cement off the strut and it ends up on the outside, to be cleaned up later. Then do the same with the other strut. If you use liquid cement, put the struts in the sockets and apply cement to the joints with a brush. This may remove a little paint, though, or leave circles that will have to be touched up later.

Immediately pick up the model and, holding the fuselage center line vertical, sight from the front to make sure the landing gear is perpendicular. Then, sighting from the side, make sure both landing gear struts have the proper — and perfectly identical — forward rake.

You may have to sight each way several times, because when you make a perpendicular correction you knock the forward rake out of line, and vice versa.

Once you're satisfied with the alignment rest the wings on a couple of books outboard of the landing gear and let the cement set overnight. Don't touch the gear or test it; just let it set. This is one of the most important steps

On many tail-dragger kits the first step in final assembly is cementing the completed engine inside the cowling.

(Top) To prevent smearing when the strut is inserted, place tube cement inside the landing gear socket, not on the strut itself. (Above) Sight the landing gear from front and sides to ensure proper alignment. This is important.

(Above) When the struts are properly aligned, rest the model's wings on supports overnight so that the gear dangles. That way, the weight of the aircraft can't make them shift. (Right) When the strut joints have dried, cement the wheels on, align them, and again support the model on its wings until the cement dries.

in final assembly, because cockeyed landing gear will make all your other carefully aligned assemblies look cockeyed, too.

In the morning your model will be able to support itself for the first time on sturdy struts, but you can't stop for that: It's time to add the wheels. If you masked the strut axles before painting, remove the tape. If not, scrape off the paint. Pull the plugs out of the axle bushings in the wheels, then put tube glue inside the bushings and slip the wheel on the axle, or put the wheel on the axle and touch it with a drop of liquid cement.

Now align the wheels as carefully as you did the landing gear struts, sighting from the front for vertical alignment and from the bottom to prevent toe-in or toe-out.

Cement the tail wheel in place if it's not molded in or hasn't been previously installed. Turn the model right side up and rest the wings on the books again while the wheel joints dry overnight. There's no rush, is there?

Canopies. The next day, install the canopy. If you have a one-piece canopy, lay a tiny bead of white glue on the paint along the seam edge, and set the canopy gently in place. If you apply too much glue or you misalign the canopy during installation and get glue inside the cockpit, pull the canopy off, wash off the glue from fuselage and canopy, and try again. White glue left inside would dry to an obvious shine.

If your canopy has two or more sections use the same technique for each part. If you mount the canopy closed you may have to apply white glue to the seams between parts to seal them, but you would be wise to mount the canopy open so you can get inside to dust during the years of shelf life ahead. Give the white glue at least a half day to set, more if you can wait.

If there are large gaps between the canopy and the fuselage continue applying white glue with a toothpick until the gaps are filled. Wash away the excess with a damp tissue after each application. When the glue has dried thoroughly, paint over it.

Wheel well doors, guns, and antenna masts. Scrape the paint out of the sockets and off the mounting pins on the landing gear struts — or remove paint from whatever means of mounting the kit manufacturer provided — and cement the wheel well covers in place. Use tiny drops of tube or liquid cement, trying not to get any on the painted surfaces.

Gun barrels can be cemented in place now, if molded separately, as well as antenna masts. Use the same technique you used for installing the landing gear and wheels: Scrape off paint from the surfaces to be joined, then put tube cement inside the hole and slide the mast or barrel into place, or slip the part into place first and touch liquid cement to it with a brush.

Aligning these small items is difficult; like landing gear, they can be off in either of two directions, or combinations of both at the same time. If misaligned, they destroy the appearance of your model. Sight from the nose to align the antenna mast with the vertical fuselage center line; sight from the side to align it perpendicular to the longitudinal center line from nose to tail.

Gun barrels should be aligned parallel to the fuselage center line when sighted from above, and parallel to a line through the thickest section of the wing chord when sighted from the side. The single cannon barrels in each wing of a late-model Zero are difficult enough to align, but you'll have a ball aligning the eight .50-caliber guns on a Thunderbolt.

If any molded-in antennas or gun barrels were broken off during construction and painting, now's the time

(Top) Align antenna masts with the fuselage vertical center line. Gun barrels (above) should be aligned with the fuselage center line when sighted from above, and with the wing chord center line when sighted from the side.

to replace them. It's nearly impossible to achieve a glue joint that doesn't show if a small broken part is simply butted and cemented, so it's best to make a new part from sprue. Cut off any remaining stump of the old gun barrel or antenna mast, drill a hole and fit the new part in it, and cement in the new piece just as if it had always been intended to be a separate part.

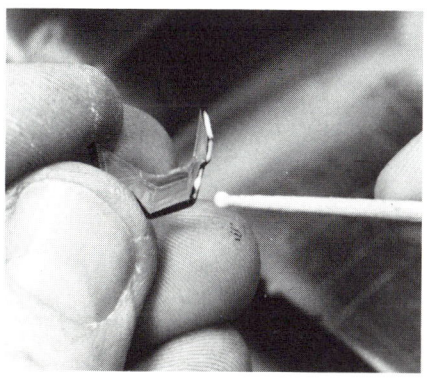

(Above) Apply white glue to canopy clear parts with a toothpick, then (right) when the canopy is firmly in place, use a toothpick to fill the seams between the painted and clear parts with white glue.

33

Remove masking or scrape off paint from the mounting pins, then attach wheel well doors. (Model and photo by Bob Angel.)

To keep its delicate blades out of harm's way during other final assembly steps, mount the propeller last.

Adding the propeller. Last of all, attach the propeller. To attach it any sooner would be to put propeller blades in the way of every operation involved in final assembly.

Some kits have a separate propeller shaft that protrudes through the gear case and is installed at the time of engine assembly. Most, however, have a shaft molded on the back of the propeller that plugs into a hole in the engine gear case. Of course you ignored any instructions early in the game to attach the propeller at engine assembly time so that it could spin freely.

While a free-spinning propeller is not a high priority among serious plastic model aircraft builders, a properly aligned one is. Few if any plastic engines have propeller shaft bushings tight enough to accomplish both goals. A free-turning propeller shaft, either type, usually includes enough slop to make the propeller hang at an angle to the center line of the engine, which looks awful. For proper propeller alignment the shaft must be cemented in place, in the case of the separate shaft when the engine is assembled, and in the case of the molded-to-propeller type during final assembly. In either case, remember to put cement in the hole first and slide the shaft into it.

Touching up. That's it. Your model is assembled. All that remains to be done is some inevitable touch-up work. With any luck, none of it will involve painting with colors, but sometimes that can't be avoided. Brush painting is the easy way out for touch-ups, but

Bob Angel built this Johan 1/72 scale P-47 Thunderbolt as an "out-of-the-box" project.

brush marks may show if the model has been airbrushed. Airbrush touch-ups can be done, but only with the most careful and tedious masking to keep overspray off canopies, contrasting areas, and markings. No masking tape must touch decals, or they may be pulled off. If decals must be masked, cover them with tissue.

If you were careful with cement, the only touch-up you'll need to do is spray or brush some clear flat finish on the spots where small exposed areas of cement have dried shiny.

Once the flat has dried, you've done it. You've completed roll-out. Rock back in your chair and admire your work. You've just completed your first successful out-of-the-box model. Call in your parents, your wife, and your friends, tell them to keep their hands off — the propeller doesn't spin — and have a look at what you've done. The uninitiated will say "that's nice," and walk away wondering why you wasted your time on a toy like that. But the modelers in the bunch will compliment you, and perhaps even ask about your technique for something that catches their eye. You'll feel like you have arrived in model building circles — and you have!

Set your model where it won't get knocked to the floor, but where you can see it and admire it. It may be anywhere from 24 hours to three days before you'll be ready to start another one.

With a few low-wing fighters under your belt you're ready for challenges like these. (Above) An Artiplast (now out of production) 1/48 scale Supermarine Walrus biplane, (below) an AMT Gloster Meteor with tricycle landing gear — and weighted nose — and (right) a multiengine Monogram B-25J.

8 Tricycle landing gear, jets, multiple engines, and biplanes

New tricks for non-tail-draggers

If you're like most modelers, you won't build many single-engine tail-draggers before you'll want to tackle some other type of plane: a jet, perhaps, or a multiengine bomber, or a biplane.

The basic techniques you learned while building your first model apply to all these types. But now you'll face new challenges: Choosing a jet or a multiengine job just about guarantees that you'll be working for the first time with tricycle landing gear; building a biplane means setting an extra wing up on a "hat rack."

Installing tricycle landing gear. All but the earliest jets have tricycle landing gear, and almost all multiengine aircraft used by the United States during World War Two — major exceptions being the Boeing B-17 Flying Fortress, Curtiss C-46 Commando, and Douglas C-47 Skytrain — were similarly equipped.

Working with tricycle landing gear isn't difficult, but it does require pre-planning and extra effort. When you tape together the major parts of your first tricycle-geared model you'll discover that, unless the plane is a modern jet with the main gear far to the rear, the model will fall on its tail. You could remedy this by holding the tail up with a crutch, but this, to say the least, would be unrealistic and unacceptable.

The solution is to add weight to the nose of the model until there's more weight forward of the main gear than behind it. This is easy enough in a jet or fighter or fighter-bomber with an enclosed nose — you can hide all the fishing sinkers, .45-caliber slugs, or whatever weights you choose in the nose and they'll never show. With a glass-nosed bomber it's a different story; you'll find yourself looking for every possible place to hide weight.

You'll want to use as little weight as possible so as not to overload the landing gear (bowlegged aircraft never get off the ground in a contest), and the farther forward you put the weight the less you'll need. While your model is

35

Here's the "why" of nose weights for aircraft with tricycle landing gear — without weights, this taped-together B-25 would have to wallow along on its tail skid.

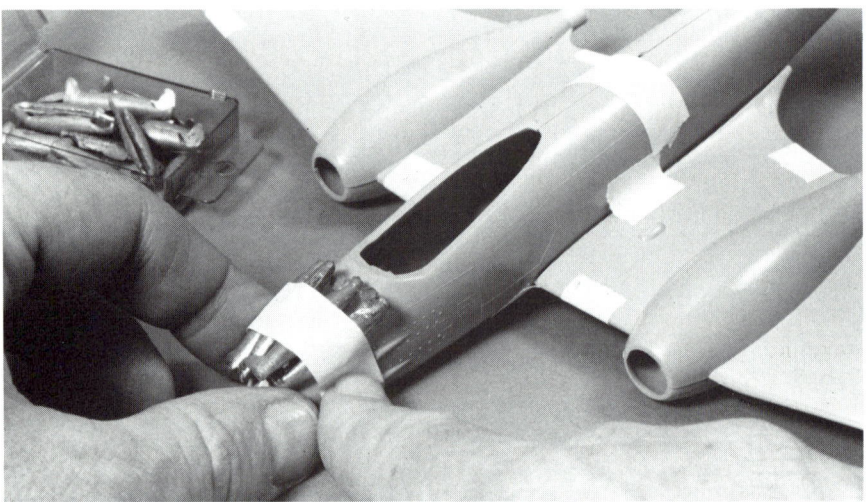

To determine the required nose weight, fishing sinkers (above) are taped one at a time to the nose of a Gloster Meteor until it stays down. (Below) Lead shot is spooned into a plastic box taped to the nose of a B-25 to shift the balance point toward the tail.

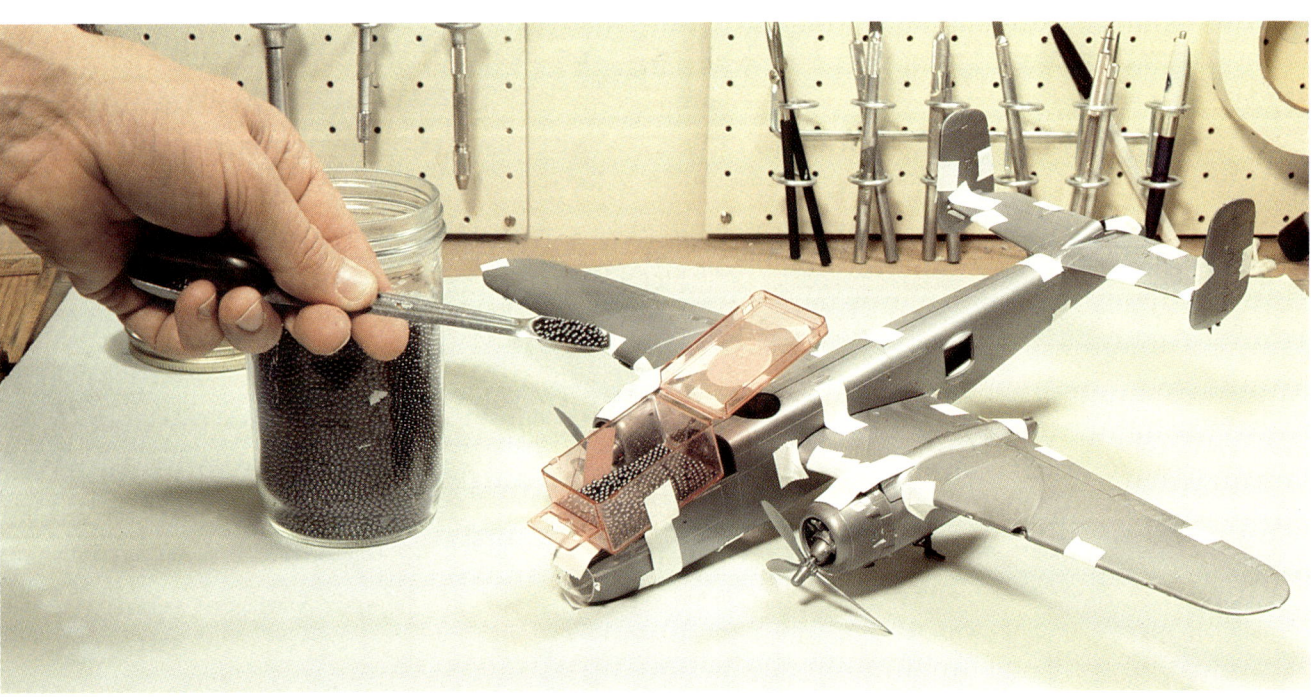

still taped together, establish a balance point where the main gear axles will be. Tape the main gear in place if it can be done solidly enough not to move when weight is added.

If your model has an enclosed nose, start taping weights to the outside of the fuselage near where they will be hidden inside. When the model goes over center and the nose stays down, add a little more for insurance.

On a glass-nosed bomber, tape a small plastic box to the nose and pour in the finest bird shot you can get (gun shops sell it by the bag) until the nose stays down, and again add a little extra.

Now you know how much nose weight your bomber needs; you just don't know where to hide it. The fact is, weight can go almost anywhere. Mixed with epoxy, fine bird shot fits into a lot of places other types of weight won't, and you'll find yourself considering every hollow part forward of the main gear. On 1/72 scale models try filling a hidden radio compartment or a closed bomb bay with shot; in 1/48 scale, ammo boxes, bombsights, seat bases — even nosewheels, if they have hollow halves — are fair game. If these small areas won't hold all the weight you need, you'll have to engineer false cockpit floors, double bulkheads, and nosewheel well ceilings and sandwich shot between them to hold the remainder.

Preplanning and weighting done, set the weight aside where it won't be lost or spilled and proceed with the first steps in fuselage construction.

Introducing new glues: cyanoacrylates and epoxies. On a model with an enclosed nose build the fuselage interior as you normally would, but stop short of cementing the fuselage halves

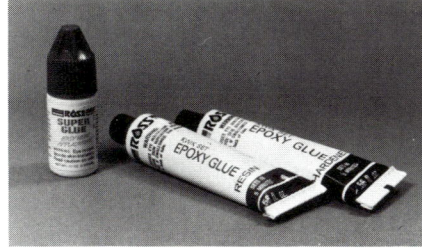

You'll need special adhesives to bond metal to plastic. Super glue works well for attaching solid weights; epoxy is good for mixing with lead shot.

Hidden areas in this B-25 cockpit have been boxed in with sheet styrene. Here the boxes are being filled with a jam-like mixture of epoxy and fine lead shot.

together. Now is the time to cement the nose weight inside, and now is the time when an item from your "nice to have" list of tools and construction materials shifts over to the necessary list. You must decide which it will be: a cyanoacrylate cement (super glue) or 5-minute epoxy.

Super glue will do an almost instantaneous and permanent job of holding large individual weights in place, and such weights are probably what you'll use in an enclosed nose model.

Epoxy takes a while to set, but it can do double duty. It can be used to hold large weights in place in enclosed noses, and it can be mixed with small bird shot and the mixture buttered on bulkhead "sandwiches" or into the nooks and crannies of a glass-nosed bomber.

Use your choice of adhesive to install the weights. Once they are solidly attached, trial fit the fuselage halves. You may have to file the weights to make the fuselage seams touch again.

When the fit is restored cement the fuselage halves together in normal fashion, but be aware that the completed fuselage will be extremely nose heavy and awkward to handle. Because of this, the fuselage can easily be dropped — and will always land nose first because of the added weight inside. Seams may be split, plastic broken, and cockpit components jarred loose, making all sorts of repair work necessary. Be careful.

Tips for building jets. Other than going through the procedure for balancing the plane on its tricycle landing gear, you'll find building a jet fighter or fighter bomber no different from building a propeller-driven aircraft. In fact, it may be simpler. There's no engine or propeller to fool with, and the thinness of jet wings and tail surfaces just about guarantees they'll be molded solid, so there are no halves to cement together. Thin parts tend to warp, however, so you may find yourself at the stove slaving over a pot of 180-degree water to straighten them.

Painting will probably be the only area where you will find jets a greater challenge than your first two-color tail-dragger: Many jets are painted three or more colors. If the paint schemes have feathered edges, freehand painting these for the first time will be a learning experience, to say the least. If the colors have hard edges you'll need lots of time and masking tape.

Building multiengine aircraft. Kits of World War Two-era multiengine, propeller-driven military aircraft take longer to build than the single-engine variety simply because there are more parts. A North American B-25 Mitchell, for instance, has two engines and two vertical stabilizers; a Consolidated B-24 Liberator has four engines and two vertical stabilizers.

Most bombers, both medium and heavy, have fuselage components far more complex than the simple cockpit of a fighter, including many more clear parts. For starters there's the glass nose, which allows the bombardier's and navigator's gear to be seen inside; then there are nose, top, bottom, and tail turrets, as well as waist gun positions, each with appropriate armament; and finally there's a variety of small windows. The bomb bay is yet another complication, but is easily dealt with on your first bomber: Simply build the model with the bomb bay doors closed.

Fitting clear parts will add many hours to the project. Butt-jointed glass noses, such as on Martin B-26 Marauders, early-model B-24s, and B-17s can be flat-sanded like a fuselage half, but don't remove much material or you'll reduce the size of the tapered clear parts and create offsets between them and the fuselage. Other types of noses, those with a variety of angles and surfaces, must be sanded with sandpaper wrapped around a wood block. The same is true for non-turret tail gun po-

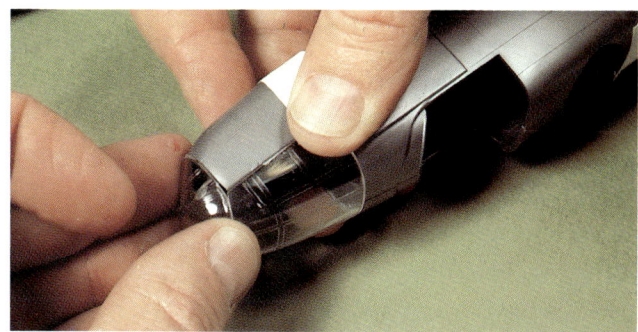

(Above) Clear parts for bomber noses require careful fitting, and interior details that will be visible through them, like this gun turret assembly (left), must be painted before assembly.

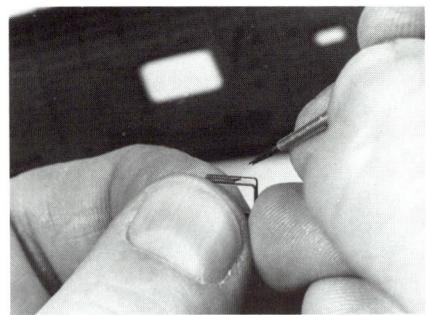

Paint the edges of small fuselage windows before installation to help hide their overscale thickness and plastic shine.

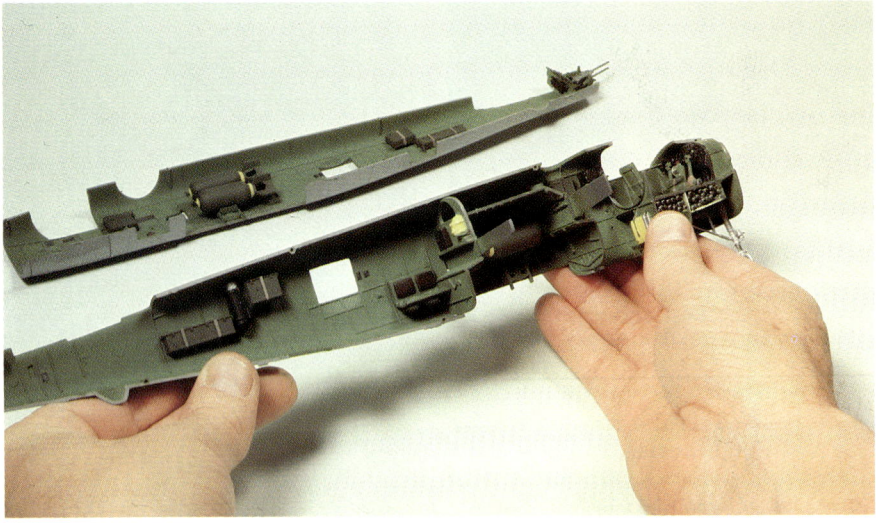

A completed B-25 fuselage interior with all components in place, including the hidden cockpit compartments filled with weight. The next step is assembly.

sitions. On bombers with "greenhouse" noses the clear parts are fitted similar to the canopies on older, non-bubble-canopy fighters.

Simple turrets that glue directly to the fuselage on 1/72 scale models can be flat-sanded on the bottom, but the more complex rotating turrets on some 1/48 scale models are construction projects in themselves. Refer to the kit instructions for assembling these, and also for the proper time to fit them into the fuselage: Some must be installed before cementing the fuselage halves together.

With few exceptions, all clear parts, once fitted, are held for attachment at final assembly. The most common exceptions are small windows that must be glued into the fuselage before the halves are cemented together. Install these after the interior of the fuselage is painted. They must be cemented solidly to keep them from being pushed in during subsequent handling, because after the fuselage is sealed they are impossible to reach.

Before installing such interior windows paint the edges of the clear plastic with exterior color to hide their overscale thickness. If the windows have a flange, scrape away the interior paint so you can glue plastic to plastic, then tack the corners inside the fuselage with tube cement or super glue, using tiny drops so as not to fog the clear plastic. No flange? Do the best you can, again tacking the corners with cement, keeping in mind that you'll need to leave a small frame around the outside of the window when you mask it for exterior painting. This frame will help hide the discoloration caused by the cement.

If the edges of the windows can be seen inside the fuselage after assembly, fill the remainder of the gap between clear and colored plastic with white glue, and when dry, touch up the paint to cover the areas scraped off earlier.

When you're satisfied that all the clear parts are solidly attached, glue in the completed interior components — seats, instrument panels, bombs, bulkheads, and weights, if you haven't done so already — sweep up, take a last look around, and cement the fuselage halves together.

Tail surface variations. Tail surface assembly on single-fin, multiengine aircraft is about the same as for single-engine fighters. On 1/72 scale models the tail surfaces are usually molded solid, but in 1/48 scale they are almost always molded in halves, and are large enough to be flat-sanded and cemented with an eye toward removing warps, just like wings.

For twin-tail aircraft the assembly procedure becomes more complex. B-24s and B-25s, for example, have twin vertical stabilizers, one at each end of a one-piece horizontal stabilizer that rests in a cradle across the top of the fuselage. The slightest difference in height of the cradle on either fuselage half will tilt the horizontal stabilizer in relation to the fuselage, so you must file or sand the cradle level.

To further complicate matters both aircraft have a fillet at the front where the stabilizer meets the fuselage. Trimming the cradle may drop the stabilizer fillet below the level of the fuselage and require a putty job to build it up. You have to decide whether it is easier to match the fillet and one side of the cradle-stabilizer joint and putty in the resulting crack on the other side, or to level the stabilizer on both

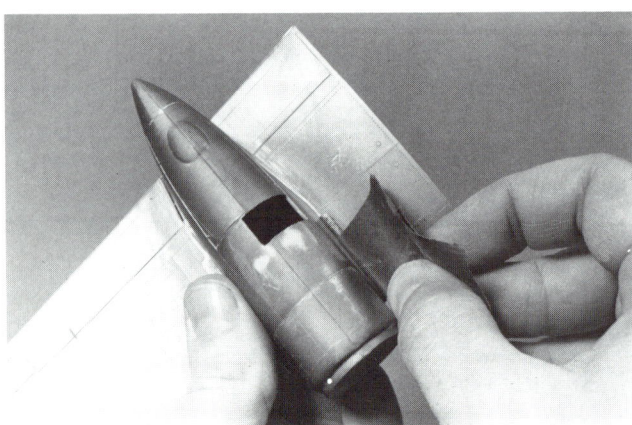

A paintbrush handle with fine sandpaper wrapped around it makes an excellent sanding tool for fairing the seams of an engine nacelle smoothly into the wing.

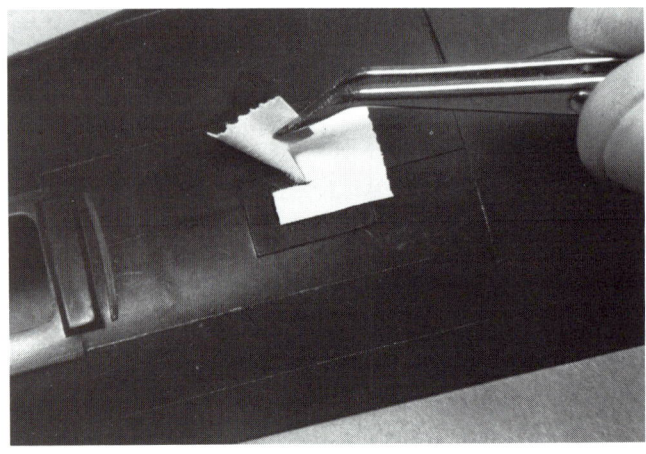

Care must be taken not to dislodge small fuselage windows when masking them prior to painting the fuselage exterior.

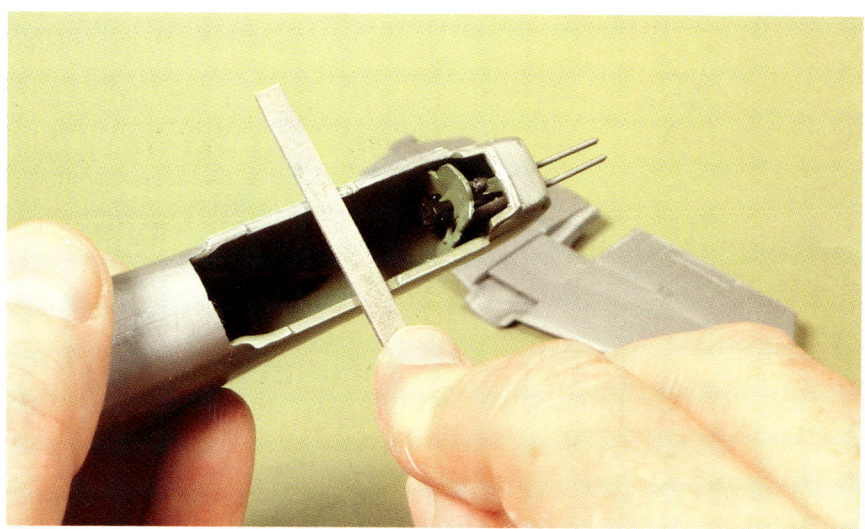

This cradle for a one-piece horizontal stabilizer is carefully leveled with a file so the alignment of the completed tail assembly will be correct.

sides of the cradle and build up the fillet.

Seldom are the twin vertical stabilizers themselves a problem. They simply butt against the ends of the horizontal stabilizer, and usually can be fitted perfectly with a few strokes of a file or sanding block.

Wings and engine nacelles. Assembling the wings of a multiengine model is basically the same as for single-engine types. Flat-sanding and warp removal are identical, but wing assembly is complicated by the need to fit two or four engines, propellers, and cowlings — and engine nacelles, too, if they aren't molded into the wing. Most World War Two multiengine aircraft had their main landing gear enclosed in the inboard engine nacelles, further complicating the situation.

Some models have portions of the engine cowlings molded into the nacelles, which are in turn molded into the wings. With these, engines must be installed before the wing halves are cemented together; others call for the main landing gear to be installed before a separate nacelle is attached to the wing.

Before assembling the wings and nacelles of any multiengine model read the instructions carefully to see if landing gear, engines, and other components must be fitted into the wing halves before the seams are sealed. This is not too likely on 1/72 scale models, but is often the case in 1/48 and larger scales. If so, the components must be cleaned up, painted, and cemented in place before final wing assembly.

While some nacelles are one-piece items that are easily cemented to the wing, most have two parts. Assemble these just like miniature fuselages, sanding the seam edges of the halves flat and then cementing the halves together — around any interior parts that must go in first, of course.

If painted areas inside the nacelle will show on the finished model, your last — or at least best — shot at painting them will come before the nacelle is mounted on the wing. It's much simpler to brush or spray through the large hole in the top while the nacelle is still a separate unit than to attempt to reach in through the front or the landing gear opening later, possibly with engines and landing gear in the way. Remember to paint the area on the bottom of the wing — which becomes the top of the nacelle — the same color as the inside of the nacelle. If nacelles are molded into the wings, paint the interior of the wings the proper color before joining the halves.

Most separate nacelles attach to the wings without fillets, but a few are filleted. Either way, fitting the nacelle to the wing is a challenge. Nacelles usually require sanding or filing at the edges for a perfect fit, or seams must be puttied when a perfect fit can't be achieved any other way.

After the nacelle is cemented to the wing and seams are filled, touch-up may be needed on the nacelle interior to cover areas where cement seeped in and lifted the paint. Once this is done, mount the wings to the fuselage using the same techniques (and the same care) you did with your single-engine monoplane.

Painting the exterior of an assembled multiengine airframe is the same as painting a single-engine fighter, there's just more of it — more cavities to be stuffed and more areas to be masked. Be particularly careful when pressing masking tape over small windows to avoid pushing them in. In most cases there's no way, short of boring a hole in the fuselage, to reach in and cement them back in place.

When the paint is dry, decals and final assembly follow, just as for single-engine models.

Building biplanes. As your interests in modeling and aviation history expand, it's inevitable that someday you'll tackle a biplane. You've probably shied away from these because they look complex, and they are. But complex doesn't mean impossible, just time-consuming.

Actually, building a biplane is like

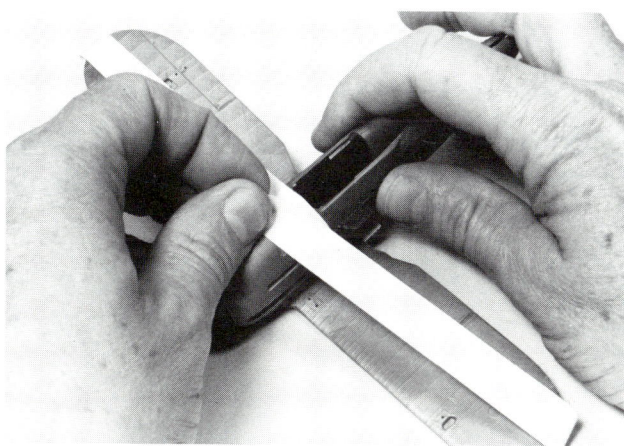
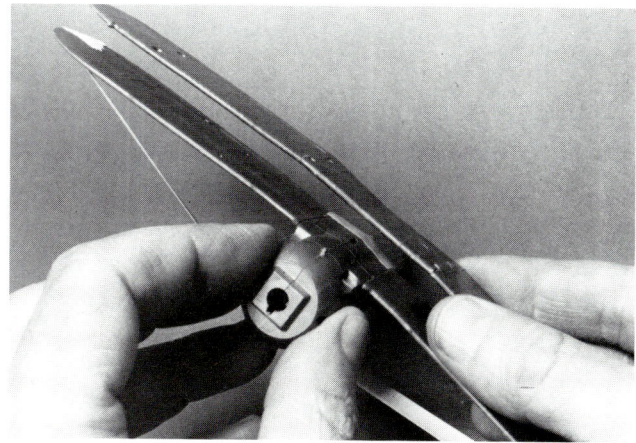

The basic construction of a biplane is the same as a low-wing monoplane; only the top wing and struts are extra. Once the correct dihedral is set in the lower wing (left), the corresponding upper wing dihedral can be set accordingly (right).

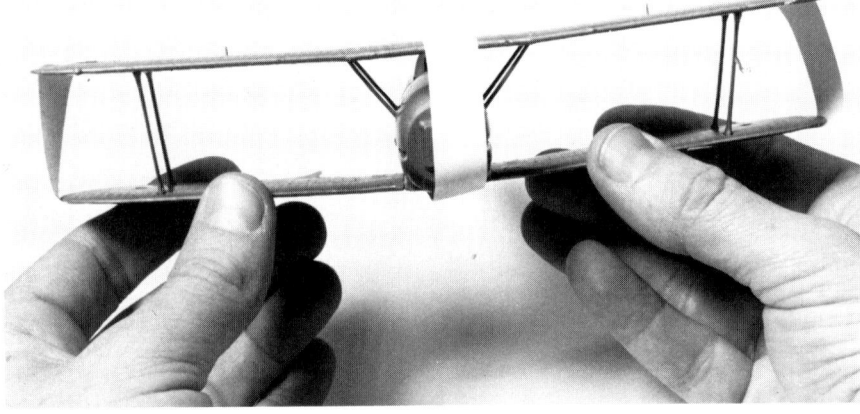

(Top) Even slightly misaligned cabane struts will result in a tilted top wing and problems in fitting the outer wing struts. To align the struts, tape the top wing to the cabane struts before they are cemented (above), insert the outer struts, then cement only the bottoms of the struts. When dry, remove the top wing for painting and reassembly later.

building a monoplane with another wing on top. Working with wing struts, the top wing, and a fixed landing gear is about the extent of the extra effort. The rest of the model is simple.

Biplane cockpits are open and uncluttered, and joints between fuselage, wings, and tail are unadorned. In fact, many World War One planes were bolted together without fairings, so unfilled seams where wing and tail surfaces join the fuselage are good representations of the real thing. On models of early biplanes the fixed landing gear can be added during final assembly as easily as you would attach retractable gear. Only on biplanes designed after 1930 will you find filleted joints and fixed, faired landing gear.

But on every biplane you eventually have to face installing the top wing. There's no secret to it — it just takes careful planning and workmanship. You'll build the model as you would a low-wing monoplane, being extremely careful to get the dihedral angles — if any — of the lower wing correct and equal, for the lower wing dihedral also influences the fit of the top wing. Too high, and the top wing will rest on the outboard struts, but not on the cabane struts in the center; too low, and the conditions will be reversed.

If the upper wing has dihedral — some World War One types were flat — and the design allows you to set it, use the same amount of care as you did for the lower wings, for the same reasons.

Once the lower wing is cemented solidly in place, remove the wing struts from the sprue trees, scrape and sand them, then tape them to wings and fuselage in their respective positions. Test fit the top wing. You may find that even after your extra attention to dihedral the wing doesn't sit quite right, perhaps because one set of struts is either too short or too long.

Here you must decide whether to shorten struts to fit or change the dihedral, whichever comes closest to yielding the correct appearance. Usually, trimming the struts is the easy way out.

When the struts fit, tape them in place and again position the top wing on them. Now sight along the model from the front to see that the top wing is positioned squarely over the bottom one and hasn't shifted to one side. When you have the top wing correctly positioned, lightly tape it to the lower wing to keep it there. Then sight from above or below to check that the leading edges of both wings are parallel. Make corrections until the top wing is in alignment from all directions, then, with it still taped in place, cement the bottoms of the struts to the lower wings and fuselage.

Don't glue on the top wing yet — even with the struts in the way, painting the main airframe and top wing will be much easier with the wing off. If you stuff tissue in the strut mounting holes in the top wing and tape the tops of the struts, cementing the wing in place during final assembly will be a breeze.

Except for some late-1930 designs, biplanes were braced in every direction with flying wires. If you want to "rig" your model, use the techniques at the end of the next chapter, which is on detailing.

9 Detailing and superdetailing

Getting in on all the details

After you've built several out-of-the-box models and are pretty good at it, you'll begin to take a greater interest in the extra details on models built by experienced modelers, the ones you see displayed in your hobby shop and featured in magazine articles.

Such details don't come in the kits, yet they go a long way toward making the models more realistic. Included are radio antenna wires; cockpits with seat belts, switches, and fancy instrument panels; wheel well hydraulic lines; and landing gear brake lines. Another detail category includes repositioned control surfaces, dropped flaps, and opened hatches, canopies, and cabin doors.

When you started building models details like these seemed far beyond anything you could ever do. Now they don't look so difficult: You could add them to your models, if only you knew what to add and how to do it, right?

Research and preplanning. If you talk to the builders of those models you've been admiring, you'll find that before they ever cut one part from a sprue tree they researched the aircraft. They bought, borrowed, or checked out of the library books and magazines that showed closeup pictures and cutaway drawings of the plane. They pored over the photos and drawings, observing every detail, searching for answers to such questions as: Were control surfaces left unlocked when the plane was parked? Were wheel well doors open or closed? Were the brake lines on the front or the back of the landing gear strut? What did the cockpit really look like?

The first step, then, is to research details. Your "nice to have" list of modeling equipment will soon include books and magazines on aircraft that interest you. After a few years of visiting your hobby shop and buying publications along with kits, you'll have a handy and valuable reference library.

How much detailing you do will depend partly on the scale in which you build. A 1/72 scale Corsair will not allow the amount of detailing that can be done on a 1/48 or 1/32 scale version of the same aircraft. Your eyesight and the steadiness of your hand also come into play, as does the amount of time you want to invest in a single model.

Personal preference determines the rest. Some modelers take the "Norman Rockwell" approach: The detailing on their aircraft is so realistic and complete that you expect the engine to start and the model to fly away. Others take an approach that's realistic but less complete: They add enough detail to raise their models well above the out-of-the-box category, but leave off the more intricate features.

Once your research has been done, you must decide, before starting to build, just what details to add or change. Some of the work, such as opening cabin doors, hatches, and gun bays, must be done while the kit parts are still in halves.

Opening doors and hatches. To open doors and hatches you'll need an item from the "nice to have" tool list, either a jeweler's saw to cut around the opening, or a hot knife — a soldering gun with a hobby knife blade mounted in it — to melt and cut its way around. Practice on scrap before you try either tool on your model, or you may find yourself going back to the dealer for a second kit.

You may want a second kit anyway, for the parts you cut out will be considerably smaller than the opening left by removing them, and filing and sanding the edges will make them smaller still. If a door or hatch cover is to be mounted wide open the difference in size won't be too apparent, but if you become a purist at this sort of thing, you'll want a perfect fit. This is achieved by deliberately cutting the part to be removed smaller than the outline, filing the outline of the opening to proper size, then cutting the door or cover oversize from a second kit and filing and sanding it to correspond to the opening.

If the door or cover is relatively flat, you may be able to save the expense of a second kit by making the part from sheet styrene, which is available in a number of thicknesses from your hobby dealer.

While the fuselage is still in halves drill and file out air intakes. Once a scoop is opened, you may be able to see daylight through it. This is unrealistic: On the real airplane there was an oil cooler or radiator or carburetor intake back there somewhere, blocking the light. To remedy the situation simply cut a baffle from sheet styrene, fit it, and cement it in place to keep light from coming through. Paint the baffle black before assembling the fuselage halves. Use the same technique for

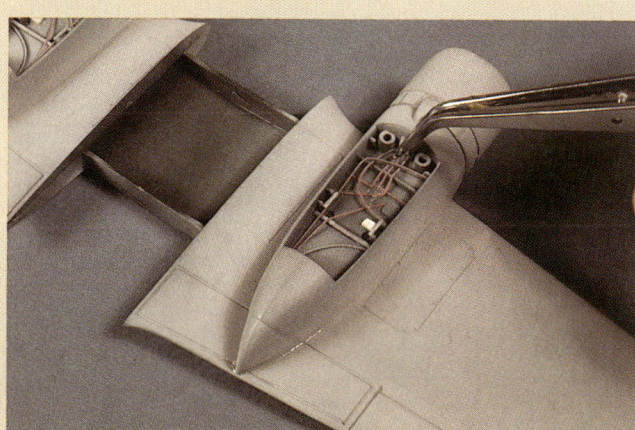
Mike Derderian simulated the hydraulic lines and electrical cables in the wheel wells of this 1/72 scale Dornier Do-217 by adding sections of thin stretched sprue.

Mountains of research material are available in magazines and books on almost any aircraft subject you choose to detail.

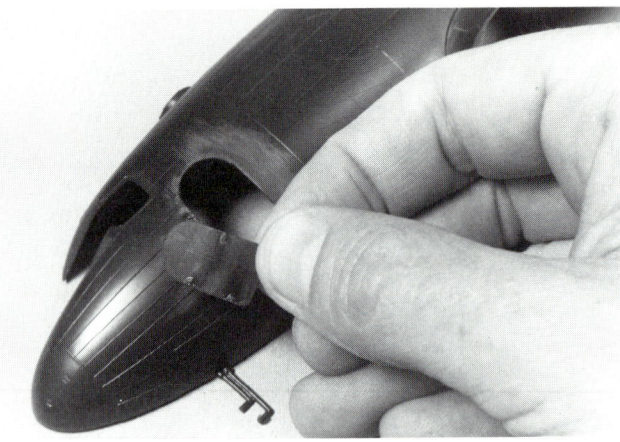

(Left) A "hot knife" (a soldering iron with a modeling knife mounted on its tip) is a big help in opening hatches, service panels, and doors. (Right) Its edges filed and sanded, the cut-out door is ready to be remounted in the open position.

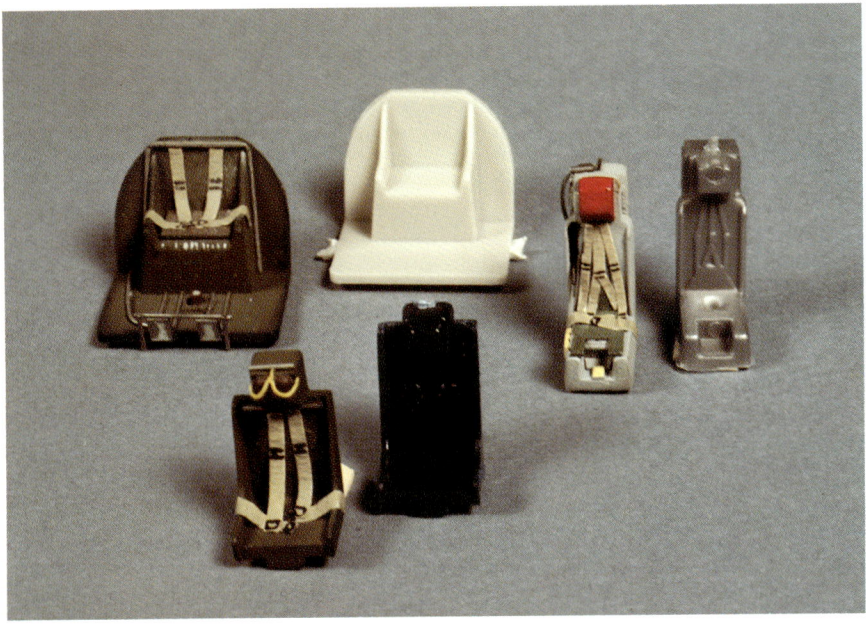

These three pairs of 1/72 scale seats illustrate how much paint and masking tape belts and shoulder harnesses improve their appearance. The original, kit-supplied seats are on the right; Mike Derderian's detailed versions are on the left of each pair.

older jet kits that have no engines or molded-in baffles.

If the air intake extends across both fuselage halves — the "built-in headwind" of the Curtiss P-40 Warhawk or the radiator cooler of the P-51, for instance — fit the baffle in both halves but cement it only to one.

The cockpit. In detailing you'll normally follow the general procedure for building the model, working with kit parts and adding the extras as you go along. The cockpit is the usual place to start, and one of the most common forms of cockpit detailing is adding seat belts and shoulder harnesses. These are easily cut from masking tape, and the metal parts are either painted on with silver paint or added using miniature fittings that you can buy.

Detailing the instrument panel usually comes next. Some kits furnish a beautifully detailed decal which needs no enhancement; others provide an exquisitely molded panel that needs only detail painting. Japanese instrument panels in particular lend themselves to

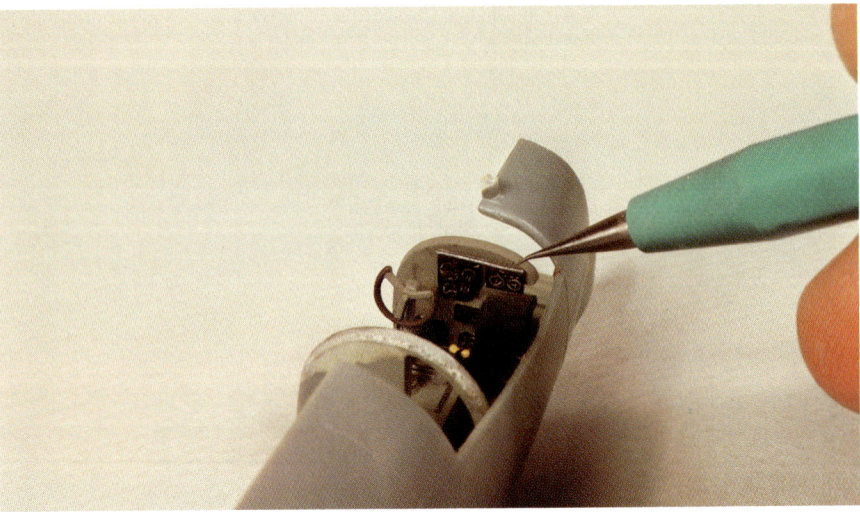

(Left) This cockpit tub from a Hasegawa 1/48 scale Zero has a hand-painted instrument panel and fuel lines made from a strand of electrical cord. (Above) Mike Derderian cut the instrument panel in this 1/72 scale Junkers Ju-86 from white sheet styrene, painted it black, then scribed the instruments with a sharp tool and a draftsman's circle guide.

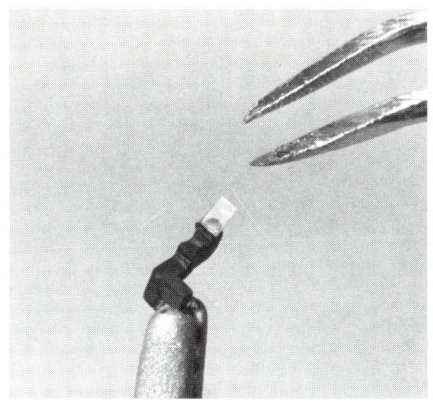

The molded-in reflector on this Zero gunsight was filed off and a rectangle of clear butyrate plastic white-glued in its place.

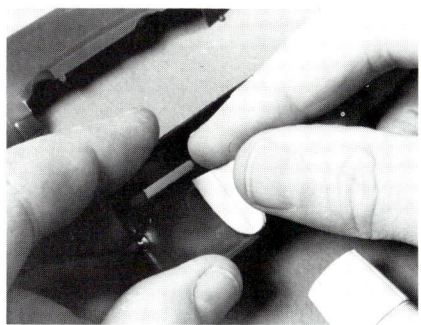

After opening the air scoops on this P-40, this simple sheet styrene baffle had to be mounted in the nose. Otherwise you'd be able to see all the way through the model from one end to the other.

ety of sizes smaller than the original.

To stretch sprue, simply heat a six-inch section over a candle flame, holding it by the ends and slowly turning it to heat it through until it begins to sag. Remove the sprue from the flame, wait a second or two, then pull gently. The sooner you pull, the thinner the filament. Pulling immediately after removing the sprue from the heat produces a result of spider web quality that's great for antenna wires. Wait longer to produce fuselage stringers and longerons to simulate welded tube steel frames. Wait longer still, and you can produce gun barrels and landing gear struts. Save your scrap sprue; it'll come in handy.

How to attach stringers inside the fuselage? If they are wood, use white glue or super glue. If they are stretched sprue, use tube or liquid plastic cement. Wherever possible, make the stringers long enough so you can glue their ends out of sight when you view them through the cockpit opening. This will help you avoid some of the greatest enemies of good detailing: glue buildup, puddling, and etching. These full-size detractors take away considerably from the effect you're trying to produce in miniature.

Since most cockpit detail parts are not under stress, use white glue whenever you can. It doesn't remove paint, it doesn't run, it dries clear, and excess can be washed off. Liquid plastic cement and super glue dry clear, but they're the reverse of everything else positive about white glue. Super glue, however, is about the only cement that will bond wire to plastic. Tube cement is easy to control, but it builds up under small parts, squishes out, dries slowly, and leaves cobweb-like strings that are difficult to see, at least until the model is on exhibit or in a contest.

Detailing engines. Aircraft engines offer detailing challenges all their own, the extent depending on the scale. On small-scale engines often all you can do is add ignition harnesses made of soft wire, and perhaps a propeller governor unit. In larger scales — particularly on models which will be displayed with the engine servicing panels removed — electric, hydraulic, and fuel lines, as well as control rods and cables can be added using soft wire and stretched sprue.

Reworking wheel wells. Detailing wheel wells on models of early aircraft with retractable landing gear may be merely a matter of enclosing them. On some early kits the wheel wells were simply holes cut in the fuselage or wing. Except for some early Navy fighters — the Wildcat was one — full-size aircraft weren't built that way. Early Me 109s and P-40s, for instance, had wheel wells enclosed with canvas, and most later aircraft had metal wheel well enclosures.

detail painting: Their artificial horizons had a blue sky, and the red-line sections of their tachometers were actually red. German Luftwaffe panels often featured instruments with bezels painted to match the color keys for fuel, hydraulic, and electric lines.

If the kit instrument panel is entirely lacking in character you may elect to build your own, using commercially available miniature instrument faces, instrument faces cut from scrap decal sheets, or by engraving faces on black-painted white plastic sheet with a circle guide and a scribing tool.

More cockpit details. From there you can go as far as you like. Try replacing the molded-in portion of a reflector gunsight with a small rectangle of thin, clear butyrate plastic, fastening it with white glue. Add radio panel fronts, oxygen regulator faces, and rudder pedals. Make panel switches, throttle and mixture controls, and seat adjustment and other handles from pins, soft wire, or toothbrush bristles. The best way to mount such parts is to drill holes and plug them in, fastening each with a tiny drop of white glue.

Make oxygen hoses from short pieces of wrapped guitar string, and fuel lines from strands of castoff electrical cord or other soft wire. Fasten the ends with super glue. Add trim tab adjustment wheels by raiding the model railroad section of your hobby shop. If the wheels are metal, attach them with super glue; if plastic, use plastic cement.

If photos of the real airplane's cockpit show the stringers that the skin of the airplane was riveted to, you may want to duplicate these on the cockpit side walls. Depending on the scale, you may be able to use HO model railroad 2 x 2 basswood lumber, fine wire, or a marvelous modeler's resource called stretched sprue.

Stretching sprue. Stretched sprue is just what the name implies. It is plastic sprue — the treelike frame the kit parts come attached to — that has been heated and stretched to produce plastic rods and filaments in an infinite vari-

The throttle and mixture controls in Mike Derderian's 1/72 scale B-17 cockpit are sections of stretched sprue with painted balls of white glue on the ends.

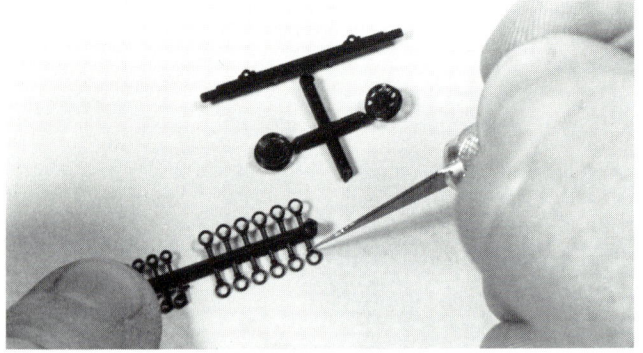
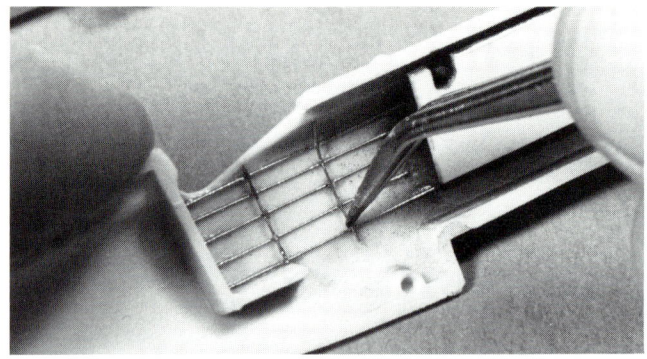

(Above) Model railroad wheels and detail parts (the items on the sprue are lift rings) make excellent trim wheels for large-scale cockpits. (Above right) When painted, these lengths of model railroad brass wire super-glued inside a 1/48 scale Macchi-Castoldi MC-72 cockpit will look like fuselage stringers. (Right) The ribs inside the hull of this 1/48 scale Supermarine Walrus flying boat are basswood HO model railroad 2 x 2 lumber. Note the use of a draftsman's ruling pen to apply Hot Stuff super glue.

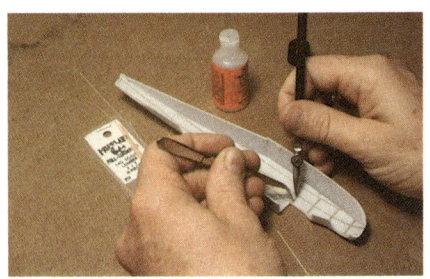

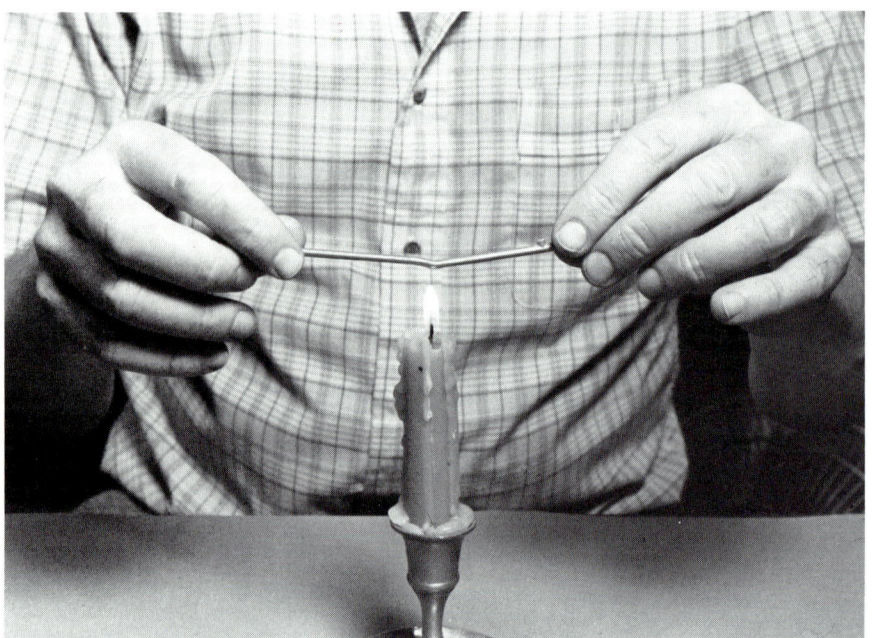

Duplicate the appearance of enclosed wheel wells by fitting a thin strip of sheet styrene against the bottom of the top half of the wing and cementing it around the edges of the opening in the lower half. The excess plastic protruding from the hole can be trimmed and sanded flush after the cement dries.

Wheel wells on every aircraft since early in World War Two feature a multitude of wiring and hydraulic lines. Kit manufacturers are molding these into late-model jets and recent kits of earlier aircraft, but most older kits cry out for you to add such detail. Use sprue or wire fastened with super glue. You can reduce the chances of winding up with a cement-soaked mess by drilling holes in the walls of the wheel well where the lines pass through.

Landing and running lights. A detailed landing light adds a lot to a model's appearance. Duplicating a round one that mounts on a landing gear or under a wing is simple: Buy a model railroad locomotive headlight lens of the right size from your hobby shop, drill or carve a recess to accept it, and fasten it with white glue after the model is painted.

The task is more complicated on aircraft with landing lights faired into the nose or leading edge of the wing. On

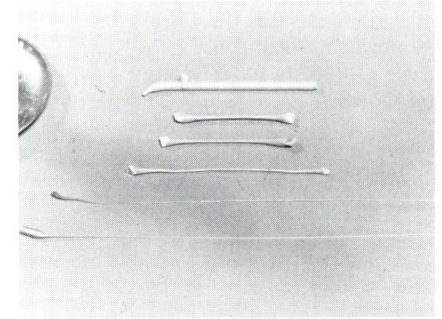

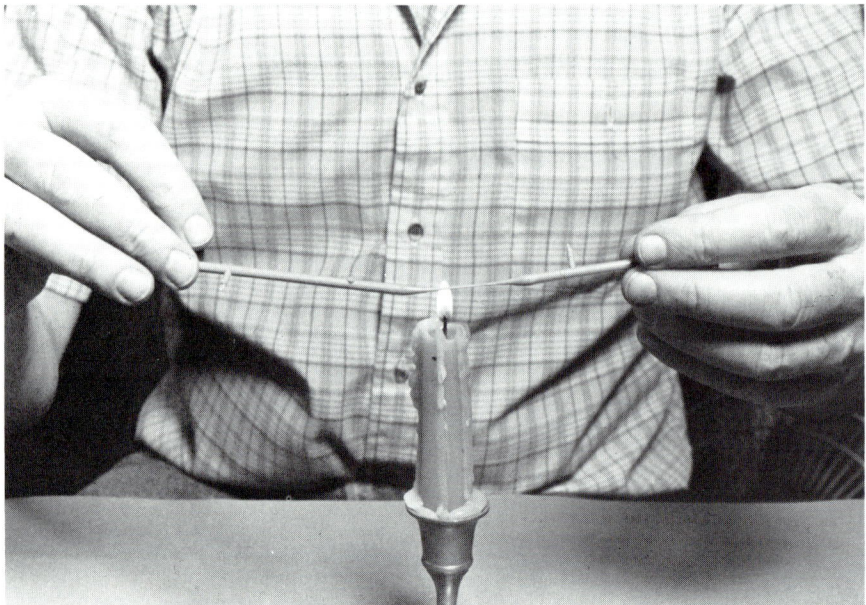

To stretch sprue, rotate a section of it over a candle flame (top) until it sags, then remove it from the heat, wait a second or more, then pull on the ends (above). The diameter of the result varies (right); the longer you wait before pulling, the thicker the result.

The original wheel wells on this 1/48 scale P-40 were merely holes in the lower wing. Thin sheet styrene was cemented around the edges, then trimmed and sanded.

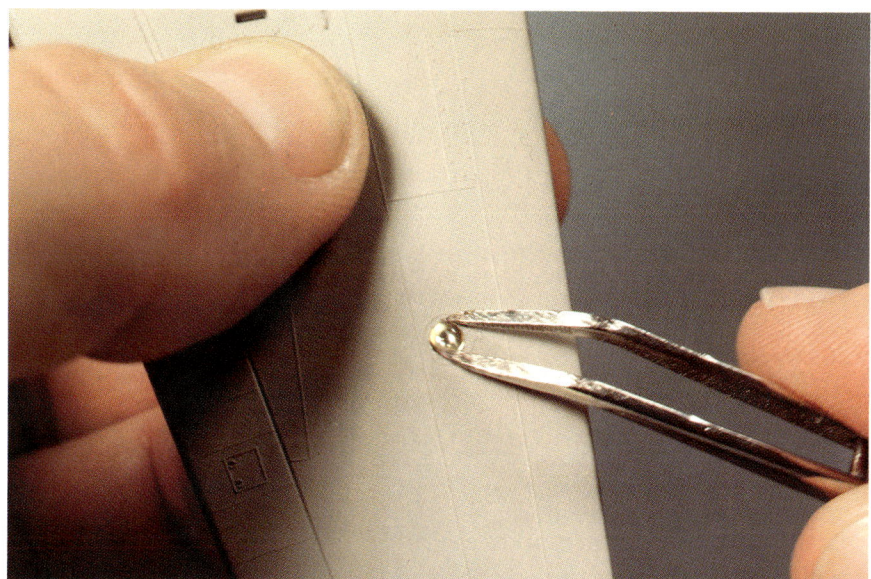

Three different ways to model landing lights: (top) a model railroad locomotive headlight lens on a 1/48 scale P-40, (center) another locomotive headlight lens tucked behind a transparent fairing in the nose of a 1/50 scale Ki-46 Dinah, and (above) a solid piece of clear acrylic plastic epoxied into the wing of a Ki-44 Tojo. The acrylic was filed and sanded flush with the surface of the wing, then polished clear. Before installation a hole was drilled in the back and filled with aluminum paint to simulate the reflector.

large models the locomotive headlight lens can be used after the light recess is cut out and boxed in. Make the box slightly smaller than the wing or nose so a clear plastic fairing can be fitted over it, flush with the surface.

On wings the fairing has a simple curve that conforms to the leading edge. A flat piece of clear butyrate can be cut, fitted, and cemented in place. On noses the curve is usually compound, and the fairing must be molded by vacuum-forming or pulling heated plastic over the nose itself or a hand-carved mold.

In smaller scales a solid piece of Plexiglas cut to fit, sanded, and polished with rubbing compound can be used for a faired-in landing light. A small hole drilled in the back and filled with silver paint simulates the reflector.

Running lights — the small green, red, or blue lights on the wings and the white light on the tail — can be painted on with gloss enamels with excellent effect on small-scale models. In larger scales bits of colored toothbrush handles can be cut, fitted, and epoxied in place, then sanded and polished to conform with the surface, yielding the transparent look of colored fairings. Running lights cut from clear Plexiglas, with a hole drilled in the back and filled with a drop of paint, simulate a clear cover over a colored bulb.

Bomb bays and gun bays. Bomb bays in recent kits offer the option of being presented open or closed, but once you're into detailing you won't be able to pass up the opportunity to open them. The kits usually come complete with bomb racks and bombs, but you'll have to add the hydraulic and electrical lines and control cables that pass along the sides and top of the bay.

With older kits and small-scale kits with closed bays you'll have to open the bay doors with a saw or hot knife, scratchbuild the bay and bomb racks from sheet styrene, add lines and cables, and scrounge bombs from your spares box, modeling friends, or both.

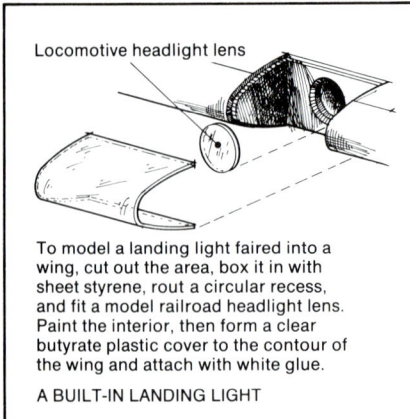

To model a landing light faired into a wing, cut out the area, box it in with sheet styrene, rout a circular recess, and fit a model railroad headlight lens. Paint the interior, then form a clear butyrate plastic cover to the contour of the wing and attach with white glue.
A BUILT-IN LANDING LIGHT

(Left) This light on a 1/48 scale Gloster Gladiator was painted with gloss enamel; the clear lights supplied in the kit for this 1/50 scale Dinah (right) were modified by filing small notches in the backs and adding dots of enamel to simulate colored bulbs.

If you open gun bays in the wings of fighters or storage compartments in the fuselage of some of the earlier fighters, you'll have to enclose the bays and compartments with sheet styrene. Preplanning will tell you if this must be done before or after the wing or fuselage halves go together.

Reworking control surfaces. When to remove control surfaces — ailerons, elevators, and rudders — for repositioning depends on whether the wings and tail are molded solid or in halves. If solid, simply saw or cut off the surfaces before the wings and stabilizers are attached to the fuselage. If they're in halves, wait until the halves are cemented together. This will ensure that the contours of the fixed and movable parts correspond.

Clean up the edges of the cuts on wings and stabilizers with files and sandpaper, and do the same for the leading edges of the control surfaces you removed. In the smaller scales simply filing the leading edge of the surface to the angle at which you want to reposition the surface will provide a good fit. In the larger scales you may want to cement a piece of styrene to the leading edge to be rounded later so that it looks like the real thing. Cover unsightly gaps in the wing or stabilizers where the control surfaces were removed with strips of sheet styrene, then sand flush.

The control surfaces can be glued back in their new positions, but often the cement will cause the natural open joint to fill in. The model will look more realistic if you drill matching holes in the leading edges of the surfaces and in the wing and stabilizers, fitting pins into them for easy, glue-free reattachment.

Full wing flaps — those that include both the upper and lower surfaces of the wing — can be handled the same as control surfaces. Split flaps — those that constitute only the lower wing surface, leaving the upper surface in place — present a challenge.

In larger scales split flaps must be cut from the bottom half of the wing before the halves are cemented together. You may have to attach simulated reinforcing strips of stretched sprue or sheet styrene to the underside of the top wing half. Cover the holes at the front and ends of the flap recess with sheet styrene, and add reinforcing strips on the upper surface of the flaps to duplicate the appearance of the full-size aircraft. If the flaps you cut from the wing are too thick, replace them with scratchbuilt parts made from sheet styrene.

On small-scale models with solid wings you can either leave split flaps up or prepare for major surgery. You'll have to cut out the whole flap section of the wing and make new parts for both the stationary upper section and the movable flap.

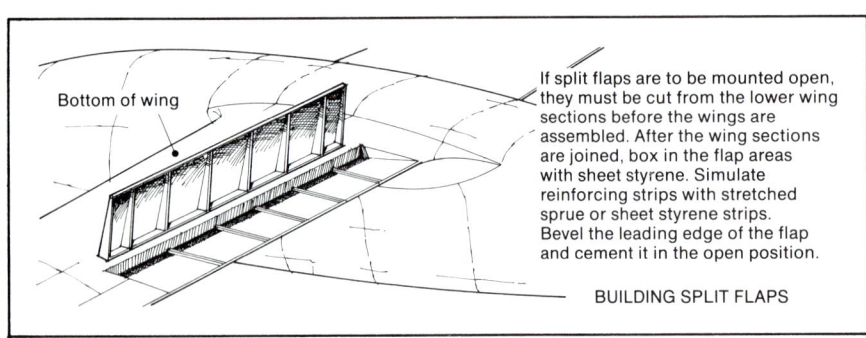

If split flaps are to be mounted open, they must be cut from the lower wing sections before the wings are assembled. After the wing sections are joined, box in the flap areas with sheet styrene. Simulate reinforcing strips with stretched sprue or sheet styrene strips. Bevel the leading edge of the flap and cement it in the open position.

BUILDING SPLIT FLAPS

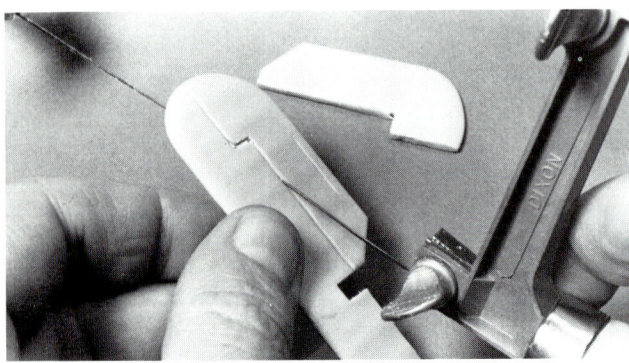
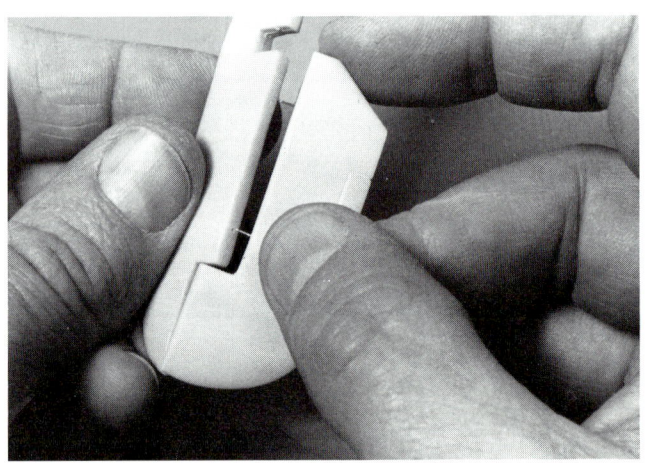

(Above) Control surfaces to be repositioned are first cut free with a jeweler's saw, then (right) reattached in their new positions with fine wire plugged into pre-drilled holes.

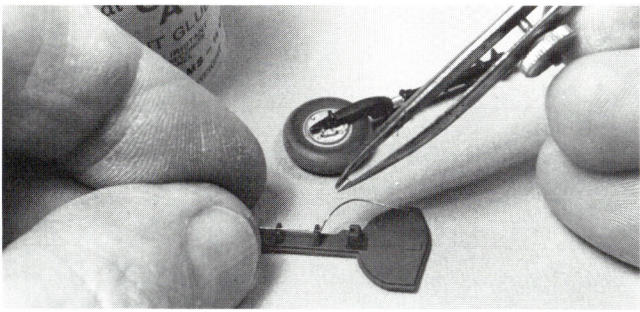 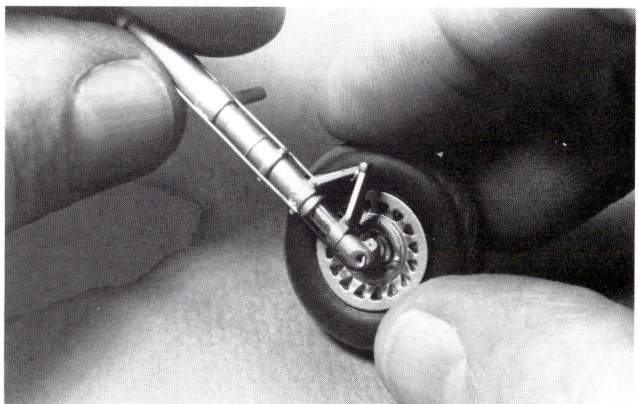

(Above) Soft wire brake lines are attached to a Zero wheel cover with super glue. (Right) Pre-drilled holes allow easy mating of brake lines and wheels at assembly time.

Landing gear detailing. In the most recent kit releases the landing gear is usually highly detailed, but in older kits that's not necessarily so. Early kit designers often left off the oleo strut hinges, which have one half on the upper and the other half on the lower portions of the landing gear to keep them in line. These hinges are easy to make from sheet styrene.

Only a few large-scale kits have brake lines molded in. On those that do not, make the lines from soft wire and fasten them to the landing gear struts with tiny pieces of tape. Make the bond permanent by touching the wire at the tape with a tiny drop of super glue. If the wheel doesn't have a molded-in brake line attachment point, simply drill a hole in the wheel at the proper spot, bend the brake line at right angles, cut it off with side cutters so that only a small peg remains, then plug the peg into the hole when the time

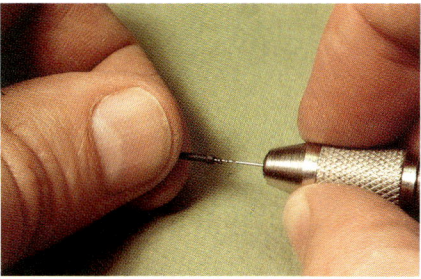 

(Left) Drilling out the bores on plastic gun barrels adds realism to the finished product, or (right) you can substitute sections of hypodermic needles. The .30-cal. barrels on this 1/48 scale Curtiss P-40 are sections of No. 22 needles.

comes to mount the wheel on the strut.

Trim the top end of the brake line so it doesn't interfere when the landing gear is mounted, but leave the line long enough so it appears to go up into the wing.

Machine guns and cannon. Solid barrels on machine guns and cannon in the small scales look unrealistic; they look ridiculous in the larger scales. Barrels can be easily drilled out with small twist drills in the larger scales, and even an indentation made with the point of a pin is enough to add realism to small-scale guns.

Small gun barrels are often poorly molded — they come out oval rather than round, or worse yet, have upper and lower halves that don't line up. If they're too small to true with a file and sandpaper, replace them with gun barrels made from stretched sprue or with hypodermic needles of the appropriate size. A No. 19 needle, for instance, is about the right diameter for a 1/48 scale .50-caliber barrel; a No. 22 needle is correct for a .30-caliber barrel in 1/48. Number 6 needles are about right for 1/72 scale gun barrels or pitot tubes for 1/48 scale models.

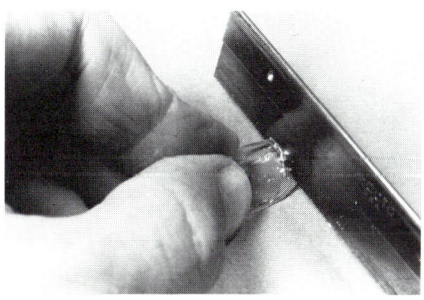

The easiest way to open a canopy is to simply cut the clear part with a razor saw.

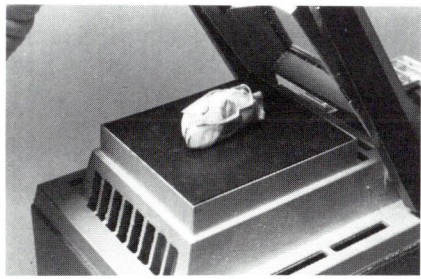

Prior to vacuum-forming a replacement over it, this kit canopy was stuffed with Plasti-Tak to raise it off the vacuum platform and allow the new canopy to conform completely to its sides.

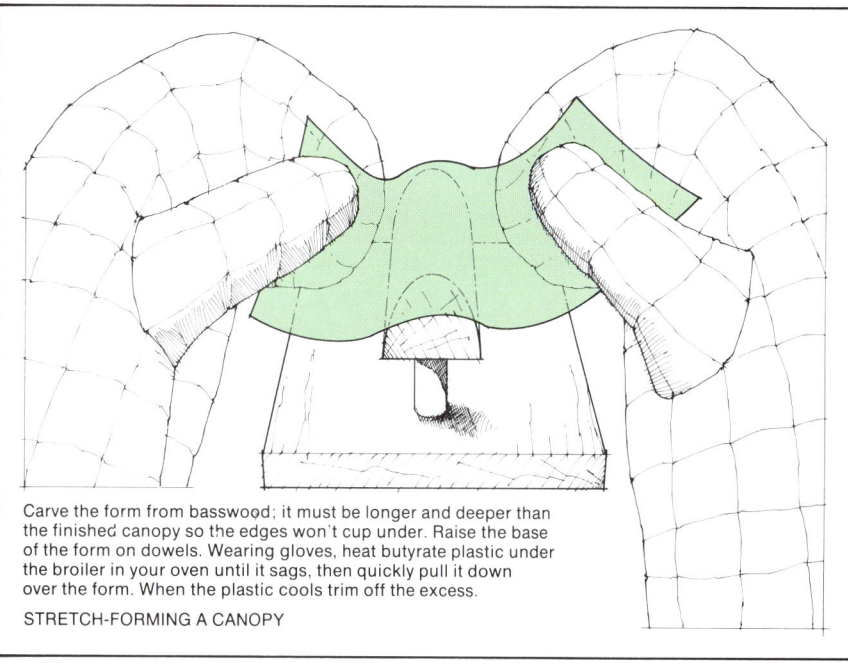

Carve the form from basswood; it must be longer and deeper than the finished canopy so the edges won't cup under. Raise the base of the form on dowels. Wearing gloves, heat butyrate plastic under the broiler in your oven until it sags, then quickly pull it down over the form. When the plastic cools trim off the excess.

STRETCH-FORMING A CANOPY

Three ways to rig biplanes: (top) a Lindberg 1/48 scale Hawker Fury rigged with nylon thread, (center) a 1/48 scale Gloster Gladiator rigged with stretched sprue, and (above) Mike Derderian's 1/72 scale Armstrong-Whitworth Siskin rigged with fine piano wire.

Either sprue or needle replacement barrels can be simply cemented in drilled-out openings in the wings of fighter planes where the receiver portions of the guns don't show. On turret-mounted and hand-operated guns in bombers the old barrels should be cut from the receivers and holes drilled so the new barrel can be cemented in. Use super glue.

Empty machine guns are acceptable in a parked bomber, but the model takes on a combat-ready look with the addition of ammunition belts. Use narrow strips of tape for the belts and add short lengths of sprue or fine wire to represent individual rounds. Small rectangular wire ties from electronics hobby stores also look like ammo belts when properly painted.

Reworking canopies. Fighters and fighter bombers with canopies left open allow viewers to get a better look into highly detailed cockpits, and allow you to reach in with a Q-tip and remove the lint that invariably sticks to the inside of the canopy. Some kit manufacturers allow you to open canopies by molding them in two or more parts. Most, however, are molded in the closed position.

Opening a bubble canopy is usually a matter of cutting with a razor saw along the line where the fixed windscreen and the sliding portion meet. To avoid scratching the clear plastic place masking tape on either side of the cutting line; the tape also serves as a cutting guide.

Canopies on models with a high spine down the fuselage — Razorback Thunderbolts or early Mustangs, for instance — don't lend themselves to being cut apart and mounted in the open position. The plastic is thick enough to cause the sliding portion of the canopy to sit too high on the spine, and the result is unrealistic.

The answer is to make a thinner canopy, either by using a vacuum-forming machine to mold a duplicate over the original, or by carving a wood form and pulling heated butyrate plastic over it. Although they have not been manufactured for many years, many Mattel Vac-U-Form machines are still around, and are constantly being bought, sold, and traded among modelers. Plans and kits are also available for making your own vacuum-former. Butyrate plastic can be bought in hobby shops, particularly shops that sell materials for radio control flying models.

If you use the original canopy as a form, first fill it with modeling clay or Plasti-Tak so it stands up off the vacuform machine base. This allows the new canopy to conform to the original all the way to the bottom, and prevents the original from being crushed and broken during forming. Take care not to heat the original part for long or it may warp.

Basswood is the best material for

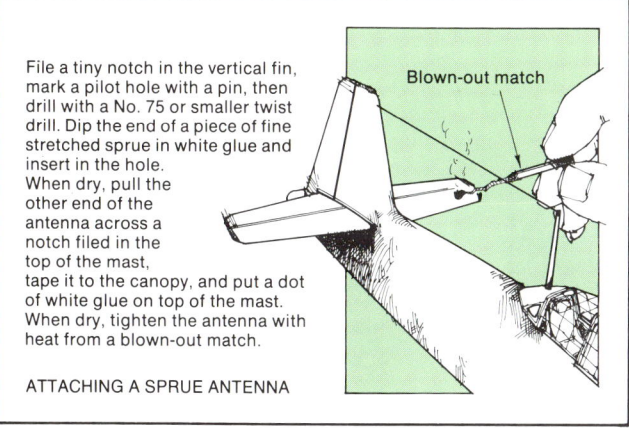

File a tiny notch in the vertical fin, mark a pilot hole with a pin, then drill with a No. 75 or smaller twist drill. Dip the end of a piece of fine stretched sprue in white glue and insert in the hole.
When dry, pull the other end of the antenna across a notch filed in the top of the mast, tape it to the canopy, and put a dot of white glue on top of the mast. When dry, tighten the antenna with heat from a blown-out match.

ATTACHING A SPRUE ANTENNA

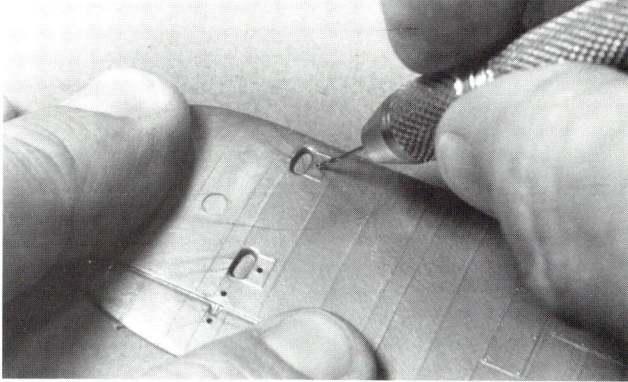

Drilling holes for rigging prior to assembly is a must.

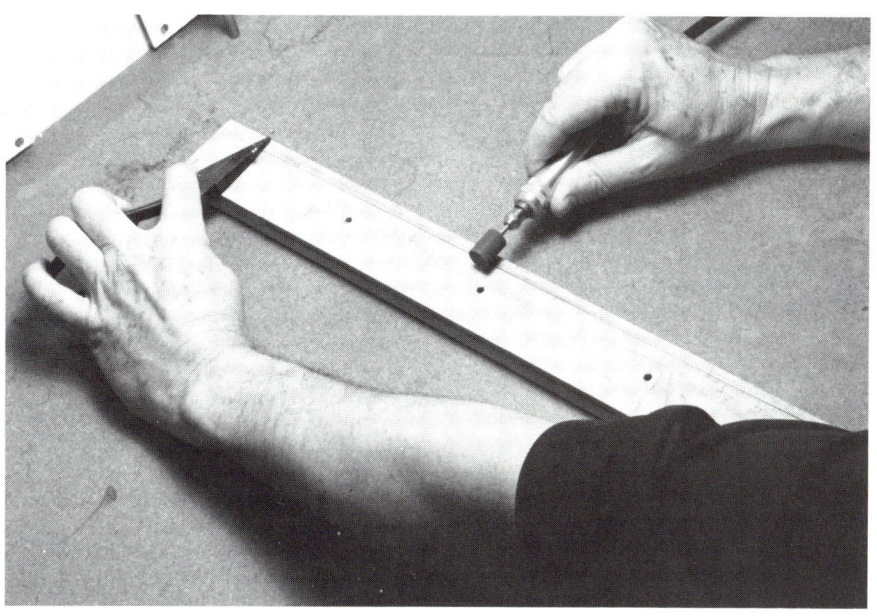

Flat flying wires for rigging large scale models can by made by grinding piano wire flat (left), then finishing it with files and sandpaper (above).

carving your own form. It's soft enough to carve easily and it's practically grainless, yet hard enough to withstand molding. The finished pattern should be mounted on a dowel which is clamped in a vise or affixed to a base so it doesn't move when the heated plastic sheet is pulled down over it.

Heat clear butyrate plastic in a common kitchen baking oven by holding the sheet (with work gloves) for a few seconds beneath the broiler unit. When the plastic begins to sag, remove it from the heat and immediately pull it down over the pattern.

If the new canopy shows wood grain, cover the form with filled epoxy from your hardware or paint store, sand smooth, clean, and try again. Whether you use the original clear part or a hand-carved form, it must be clean, because dust particles will be molded as small lumps on the new clear part.

Vacuum-forming and hand-forming techniques can be used to mold air scoops for models that don't have them, even though the scoops appear in pictures of the actual airplane, or where the molded-in scoops cannot be opened with files.

Radio antennas. Radio antennas are the last items to be added to the model because they are so delicate. They're always in the way, and are altogether too easily broken.

Antennas are easy to model using fine stretched sprue. Drill a hole in the vertical fin, if that's where the antenna wire mounts, put a tiny drop of white glue on the end of the sprue, and insert it in the hole. Let the glue dry for 30 minutes before attempting to attach the other end. Pull it tight across the top of the antenna mast (which has been filed flat, or better yet, which has a tiny V-notch filed in it) and put a drop of white glue on top of it.

If the antenna isn't tight after the glue dries, don't worry. Light a match, blow out the flame, then pass the still-warm match beneath the antenna. It will sag, then snap taut.

Rigging biplanes. Biplane rigging can be modeled with whatever looks right, including stretched sprue, thread, and wire.

Stretched sprue makes excellent rigging for small-scale biplanes. Some modelers cut pieces the proper length for a slightly loose fit between the struts, glue them in place with a dot of white glue on either end, then tighten them with the warm-match technique.

However, if the top wing receives a knock hard enough to cause it to shift slightly, those butt-glued joints may break. You can make a much stronger bond if you preplan and drill holes in fuselage, wings, and tail surfaces, and after painting and final assembly insert the ends of the pieces of stretched sprue, dipped in white glue, in the holes.

Large-scale models look better when rigged with flat flying wires like those on the full-size aircraft. You can make flat wires by grinding piano wire of the proper size flat with a motor tool, then removing grinding marks with files and sandpaper. The wire must be attached to plastic with super glue.

Once you've gotten your feet wet in the techniques of adding extra details, you'll probably find you can never build a simple out-of-the-box model again. In fact, you may find yourself advancing to the point where you aren't merely adding details, but are modifying and converting kit models into entirely different versions, then applying decals other than those that came in the kits. When you reach this point you're well on your way to joining the ranks of the world's master plastic modelers.

Congratulations!

(Above) Tom Nelson's impressive conversion of an Otaki 1/48 scale F4U-1 Corsair to a Goodyear F2G-1D displays the distinctive exhaust patterns and discoloration typical of the real plane. (Right) A severely weathered 1/48 scale Nakajima Ki-43 Oscar shows faded paint as well as considerable chipping and peeling along leading edges and panel lines.

10 Weathering

Understanding the aging process

There's one more step beyond detailing — the final step, really — to make your models into realistic miniature versions of the real thing. It's called weathering.

Weathering, in modeling lingo, means making the model look like it has been out in the weather — faded by the sun, streaked by rain, sometimes peeling and chipping. Weathering effects include stains from leaking oil coolers and the blast from short exhaust stacks, as well as dust, dirt, and mud blown back by the prop wash and thrown up by the tires.

As with detailing, in weathering research is as important as technique. You'll start by studying photos of the aircraft you're modeling to see how badly the paint faded, where it was prone to chip off, where the oil and exhaust stains were and what sort of patterns they formed, and what the mud and dirt looked like on the tire treads. Nationality is a factor here: Japanese paint faded and chipped badly; Luftwaffe colors faded some, but rarely chipped; U. S. and British colors fell somewhere in between. And in all, the amount of weathering depended on the age of the plane.

Whatever the age or nationality of the aircraft, weather with a light touch. It's easy to get carried away with weathering, and beginners often do — ending up with an aircraft so battered and worn that no self-respecting pilot would climb into it except under penalty of death! Your model will be better received by viewers and contest judges if its weathering is subtle, indicating a slightly used aircraft, but one still airworthy and capable of many more missions.

Weathering inside the cockpit. Preplanning the weathering treatment is important, for not all of it is done as the final painting step on the finished aircraft. On fighter planes with bubble canopies and bombers with greenhouse noses that admitted a lot of sun, the cockpits weathered, too. Shiny, bare-metal interiors became dull and oxidized, painted surfaces faded, black radio boxes turned shades of gray, and paint everywhere wore and chipped away. On the model, cockpit weathering must be done when the cockpit interior is being finished.

Oxidized bare metal can be simulated with flat aluminum paint; faded interior colors are simulated by adding a little white to the final coat and airbrushing heaviest on surfaces that would get the most sun. The look of chipped paint can be duplicated with small dots of flat aluminum daubed on with a brush.

Paint worn away to bare metal is best simulated by dry brushing. To use this technique, dip the brush in paint, then blot it on tissue until no paint runs out and only traces of the color remain on the brush hairs. Rub the edge of the brush on the surface to be weathered until some color sticks to it.

Another means of simulating worn paint is to put Rub 'n Buff, a metalized wax paste, on the end of your finger or a Q-tip, try to wipe it all off with a tissue, then rub what's left on the area to be weathered.

Engines that show hours. Radial engines need weathering, too. Flat black cylinder barrels turned a medium-to-dark gray from heat and water, and the shiny gray gear cases lost some of their gloss from propeller-driven dust particles and sun fading. Gray paint will take care of the cylinder color; a coat of clear flat will kill some of the gear case shine. A light touch of Rub 'n Buff on the cylinders will highlight the edges of the molded-in cooling fins and give the appearance of greater depth.

Simulating worn propellers. Prop blades weather, too. Bare metal takes on a dull, oxidized look; black paint turns medium gray and shows signs of streaking. Yellow prop tips fade, taking on a pale tone, and the paint on the

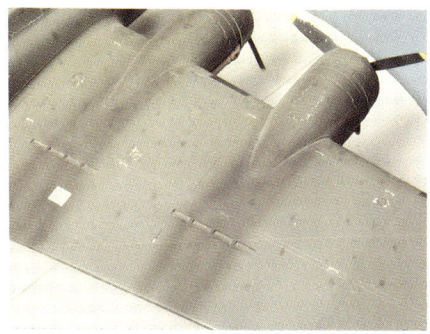

A final coat of olive drab lightened with white produced a faded effect on the wing of this B-17. Dabbing with a doubled-over pipe cleaner dipped in thinner produced the scuff marks from ground crewmen's shoes; airbrushing created the oil streaks.

(Top) The 3,000-horsepower engine in this F2G-1D has exhaust pipes burned rusty red and engine parts polished through handling. (Above) Dry-brushed aluminum paint simulates worn-off areas on the edges of seats and switch boxes, and makes this cockpit floor appear to have been scuffed through to bare metal.

leading edges erodes until bare metal shows through. Simulate fading and streaking with the techniques described below for camouflage colors, and make the bare-metal leading edges by dry brushing or applying Rub 'n Buff.

Fading and streaking for exterior paint. When the airframe of the model is finished and painted factory fresh, but before propellers and landing gear and exterior details are added, weather the camouflage colors. Fading is the easiest of all weathering techniques. As you did with the cockpit interior, simply add a little white to the final coat of upper surface color and spray it on. Spray down on the model from the top, from the same direction as the sun's rays would strike the upper surfaces.

Fading affects the wings and horizontal stabilizer most, since they are almost constantly exposed to full sunlight. The top of the fuselage runs a close second, with the fading effect lessening as the fuselage sides curve down and away from the sun. By applying whitened paint in fore-to-aft strokes that do not overlap perfectly you can accomplish a second easy weathering technique: streaking.

Fading works best on models that have a single upper surface color, but it works almost as well on multicolor upper surfaces if the camouflage patterns are masked. It makes little difference on multiple colors if the amount of white you add to one color is slightly more than another, because on real planes some colors fade faster than others. Don't attempt streaking while you fade a camouflaged scheme, however — it's impossible to match the streaks when only one color shows at a time and the others are masked.

Streak a camouflage scheme after the complete, factory-fresh paint job has been applied and the masking has been removed. Spray the upper surfaces with a thin wash of white or light gray paint, at least three or four parts thinner to one part paint. Since this will make or break your model, experi-

This Otaki F6F Hellcat's propeller was weathered by airbrushing streaks of a white wash across the blades, then dry brushing the leading edges with silver.

ment on a piece of scrap or a derelict model to get the mixture and technique right, and keep your touch light.

On cowlings, access hatches, gun bay covers, and any area on the airframe that was handled by ground crewmen the flat paint took on a slightly oily, shiny look. You can reproduce this look the same way it was made on the real plane: by touching the paint with your

(Left) Paint chipping and peeling is easily done by dotting on irregular splotches of aluminum paint with a brush. (Right) In the smaller scales, simulated chipping along panel seams looks realistic when applied with a silver pencil.

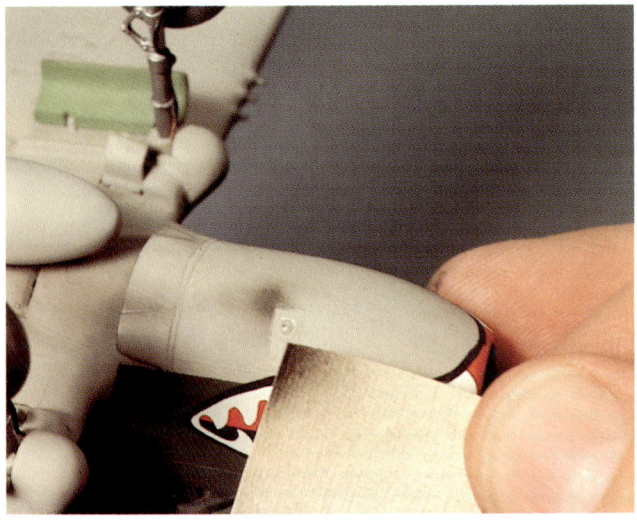 

By masking you can make oil stains appear where they should — behind oil coolers and access panels, not on them.

Exhaust pipes and surrounding areas were masked on this Otaki Ki-100 to keep exhaust residue in the proper area.

The underside of Mike Derderian's 1/72 scale Corsair shows off hand brushed oil streaks as well as carefully airbrushed exhaust smudges and gunpowder residue.

fingers. Keep your fingers moving or you'll have unrealistic, full-size fingerprints on the model. Rubbing the "oiled" areas with a Q-tip will help carry off the illusion.

Insignia and markings. National insignia are painted on the real aircraft, so they're subject to fading, too. Decals applied right off the sheet and left that way on a faded paint job won't coincide with the weathering pattern on the plane, and won't look right.

There are two ways to make decals appear faded. The first is to apply them as they come in the kit, then spray the entire plane, including the markings, with a light wash of white or gray. The second technique is to spray the wash on the markings before applying them. Cut the decal sheet apart before you do this, because all markings don't fade equally and must be weathered unequally. Upper surface wing markings fade most; fuselage markings fade more on the top half; undersurface markings fade hardly at all. Weathering the decals before application works only with oil-base paints: Anything else will wash off when the decal is soaked in water.

Chips, peels, and wear. Exterior

To achieve the dingy, weatherbeaten appearance of this 1/48 scale Ju-88 a wash of "dust and dirt" (thinned gray-brown paint) was airbrushed on its upper surfaces.

(Left) This Ju-88 C6B tire was airbrushed and hand brushed with "mud" paint to simulate running on a muddy field. (Above) This Ju-88A tire must run on a hard surface; the tread was left clean and the sidewalls were lightly airbrushed with a mud color.

paint that is chipped and peeled enough to reveal the bare metal underneath can be simulated the same way you did it inside the cockpit, by daubing tiny dots of flat aluminum paint over your weathered finish. Photos of the real plane will show where paint chipped most often. These areas usually include the leading edges of wings and tail surfaces, the fronts of cowlings, and around engine access panels and gun bays.

The only problem with daubing on aluminum paint to simulate chipping is that it can easily look like daubed-on aluminum paint. To make the chipping and fading more realistic, there's a way to do it like it really happened — from the inside out. For this technique the model must be painted with a base coat of flat aluminum before the camouflage colors are sprayed on. Flat aluminum enamel is essential here, because flat camouflage colors don't bond well to gloss metallic colors and the paint could pull off when masked over.

After spraying the factory colors over the aluminum base and weathering them, simply chip away the top layers of paint down to the aluminum with a pin. If you're concerned that the bond between colors and aluminum will be too good for pinpoint chipping, plan where the chips and peels will be and apply irregular patches of rubber cement over the aluminum paint. Then spray on the factory colors, weather them, and when dry, touch the rubber cement with a piece of tape to lift it off, revealing the aluminum beneath.

On small-scale aircraft light chipping can be duplicated by touching the point of a silver pencil intermittently along seam lines. This method offers an additional benefit: If you don't like what you've done, erase it and start over.

Simulate the foot wear patterns on the wings of fighter planes where pilots and ground crewmen stepped up to the cockpit with dry brushing or Rub 'n Buff, or, if you're brave enough, by actually wearing away the paint down to the aluminum paint base coat with a piece of worn-out 600 sandpaper.

Stains. Stains are relatively uncommon on pure jet and turbojet aircraft, except for an occasional streak from a leaking hydraulic line. But piston-engine aircraft, with their constant vibration, are susceptible to leaks around oil coolers and in the engine itself. Photos show brown-black stains blowing back from cowlings and cooler housings, mainly on the underside of the plane (engine oil runs to the bottom of the cowling, and most oil coolers are located on the undersides). Simulate these stains by painting on a light wash of the proper color with a brush, or by airbrushing the mixture with a fine tip. If you airbrush, mask the cowlings and coolers: The stains should be behind, not on, them.

One aspect of weathering was con-

Mike Derderian's subtly weathered RAF Corsair in 1/72 scale has the look of a combat-tested veteran, an aircraft that's ready for many more missions.

stantly being updated on the real airplane by the engine: exhaust stains. On the model, this weathering must begin with the exhaust stacks themselves, for the heat discoloration overrode any other type of weathering there. On relatively new aircraft the stacks or pipes burned to a multihued blue, but as the plane got older they became whiter, and finally they rusted to a dull red.

How much exhaust stain reached the fuselage or engine nacelle depended on the type of engine. The clean Rolls-Royces of Spitfires, Hurricanes, and Mustangs left only slight stains on their fuselages, light gray on dark surfaces and darker gray on light surfaces. On Messerschmitts and Junkers with inverted V-12 engines engine oil could drain down into the combustion chambers, rendering the exhaust stains an oily black. Some radial engine aircraft displayed a combination of both: dark oil stains blown back when the engine started, and light gray stains on top of them from clean gasoline combustion.

The best way to duplicate exhaust stains is with an airbrush adjusted to spray a fine line. Mask the stacks; they shouldn't show stains. Check photos for the stain pattern created by the swirl of the prop wash. Practice on scrap before you try painting stains on your model; as with any other form of weathering, overdone stains can ruin its appearance.

Dust and mud. Few World War Two combat aircraft operated off paved, hard-surface fields. In the Pacific theater they often flew from crushed coral strips and in Europe they flew mostly from grass fields. Even when planes were lucky enough to fly off a paved strip the parking areas were likely to be grass or dirt, and in all theaters there was mud, mud, mud.

As a result, the only clean combat plane was a brand new one. Veteran aircraft usually had clean windscreens simply because the pilots had to see out, but the rest of the plane was covered with a layer of dust in dry times and a fine spray of mud in wet, the amount of either depending on when the last rain fell or how recently the plane flew through a thunderstorm.

Depending on the theater the plane flew in and whether you're modeling the rainy season, you can apply a light wash of either dust or mud. Paint manufacturers produce both of these colors, but if you can't find them in your hobby shop, mix your own with light grays and browns. Dust will be heavier on the upper surfaces of the aircraft; mud will be found mostly on the undersides, and in heavier concentrations in areas where it would be thrown up by the wheels. Since mud was literally sprayed on, it's easy to simulate with an airbrush.

Weathering tires and wheels. The tread of tires operating from a hard-surface runway will be gray; those operating from a dirt strip will have a tread the color of the dirt. If the plane flies from a hard-surface runway but rolls through mud to and from its parking area, it could have gray tread bordered by a strip the color of the mud, depending on where it rolled last.

Tire weathering is best done with the wheel impaled and immobilized on a toothpick or other shaft of suitable size jammed in the axle hole, and the shaft chucked in a motor tool or other rotating device that is taped to a table or clamped in a vise. This allows you to spin the wheel and have one or both hands free.

When airbrushing hard-surface tread wear, hold a shield close to the tire to keep overspray off the sidewall and wheel. When airbrushing mud, use the shield for the tread, but back it off and allow a slight amount to reach the sidewall and wheel, as would have happened on the real plane. When combining the two, airbrush the mud first, then use the shield to apply the look of hard-surface wear.

Final assembly. After weathering the tires you can add the landing gear, which also should have a little of whatever color you weathered the underside of the aircraft with on it — the same is true of the wheel well doors — and the radio antennas, guns, and other appendages.

When you trim the last piece of excess sprue from the radio antenna — the last step in detailing — set the model on a table or shelf where you can get an eye-level look at what you've done. You should see before you a sight that will give you goose bumps: not a factory-fresh toy, but a true small-scale replica of a specific airplane, looking as it did after surviving months of combat, rain, and sun; slightly faded and chipped, but neither bowed nor bent, and still ready for many more missions.

This is the effect you set out to produce a few months ago when you began your first model, right? Well, take a bow. You've arrived.

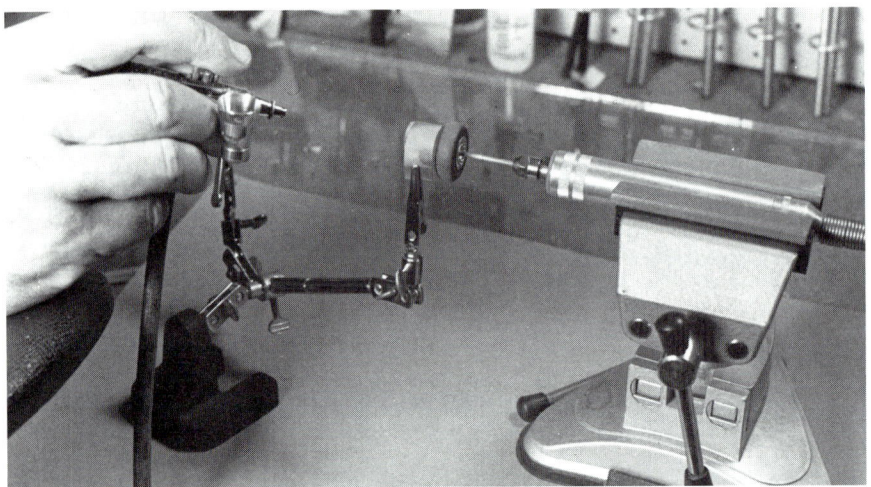

To show tread wear a wheel is impaled on a toothpick, chucked in a motor tool, and airbrushed while spinning. The curved brass strip in the clip masks the sidewall.

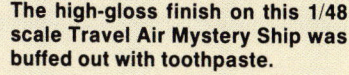
The high-gloss finish on this 1/48 scale Travel Air Mystery Ship was buffed out with toothpaste.

11 Applying gloss and metallic finishes

Taking a shine to your models

So far, all of the painting techniques in this book have concerned camouflage colors on combat aircraft. But not all combat aircraft are painted: Except for anti-glare panels and markings, many are left with their shiny, bare-metal skin showing. And not all aircraft are military: Most commercial and general aviation planes are painted in high-gloss colors, and some airliners fly with polished, bare-metal exteriors.

Achieving a good shiny finish on a plastic model is one of the hobby's greater accomplishments. To do so, the model must be flawless: Any mistake under a gleaming finish — bad seams, dirt, dust, rough spots — shows up as though spotlighted. Gloss enamels, unless given special treatment, can make a model look like a vat-dipped dime-store toy. And without special finishes and techniques, attempts to duplicate bare-metal skin often result in nothing more than unrealistic, silver-colored models.

Preparing for bare-metal finishes. The decision to apply a simulated bare-metal finish must be made before you start construction, because you must lay the groundwork for the finish. This begins with cementing all seams with super glue. There's a good chance that the metalizing paint you use will attack body putty, eroding the feather edges of puttied seams and making them look ragged under the finish. By applying one coat after another, super glue can be built up to fill seams, and when dry it can be sanded and polished like plastic — and metalizers won't even touch it.

Polishing is the next step in preparing for a bare-metal finish. Metalizers bring out every scratch or stray knife cut which might normally be covered by a flat camouflage finish. Such flaws can remain invisible even after fine sanding, but they'll show up when the plastic is polished with auto rubbing compound or metal polish. Once revealed, the defects must be sanded and polished out.

The model's entire exterior must be polished, not just the areas around the seams. You'll no doubt find scratches showing up in areas you never dreamed were touched.

Aluminum paint. The easiest metallic finish to use is aluminum-colored enamel. After applying decals such a

Floquil Old Silver was used to simulate an unpainted aluminum skin on this 1/48 scale Otaki Ki-44 Tojo.

55

Control surfaces of this P-36 were airbrushed with non-buffing Spray 'n' Plate; simulated metal was airbrushed with Testor silver and buffed after many days of drying.

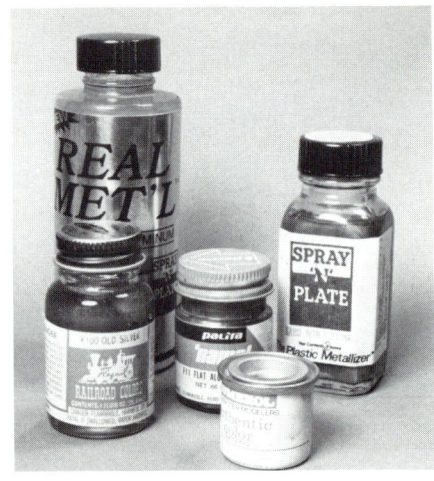

There are several types of commercial metallic finishes, ranging from oil-based enamels to lacquer-based metalizers.

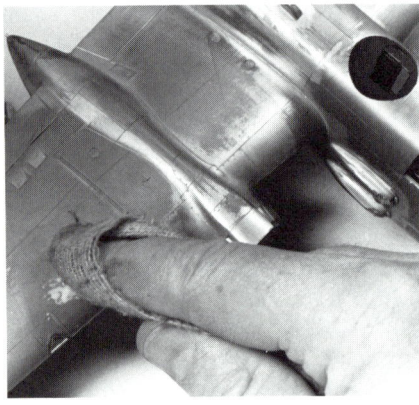

Buffing plastic with metal polish reveals imperfections and scratches that otherwise wouldn't be seen until after painting.

finish will look okay, but not much like bare metal. The main advantage of aluminum enamel is its ease of application: Simply wash the model to remove dust and lint, dry it well, thin the enamel with one part thinner to one part paint, and airbrush it on just as you would a camouflage color.

But from there on aluminum enamel offers a series of disadvantages. It takes forever to dry. It can't be masked over — the tape will pull the pigment off — so anti-glare panels and markings must be painted on and masked before the aluminum is applied. It can't be handled with bare fingers because fingerprints will etch into the finish, and it can't be handled with cloth or tissue because the cloth weave will leave an imprint on it or bits of tissue may stick to it.

Because of these shortcomings aluminum enamels are definitely the last step in the painting process: It will be weeks before the paint is dry enough for you to take any other step, such as adding the landing gear and final details.

Metalizers. Metalized finishes made specifically for aircraft modeling produce a good approximation of bare-metal skin. Some brands call for a sealer to be applied over the plastic before the metalizer is sprayed on; others say simply to clean the plastic well and polish it to a super glossy finish.

Generally, metalizers are sprayed on right from the bottle, left to dry for the time specified in the instructions — usually short — then buffed to a high sheen with a soft cloth or tissue.

Some brands offer differing shades of the same metal color to simulate the contrasting light and dark panels seen on all-metal aircraft. (The light-and-dark effect is caused either by different kinds of metal, or by the "grain" in the aluminum, which forms as the sheet is rolled. Light isn't reflected quite the same way when the grain of one piece is at right angles to another.) With metalizers, the effect is achieved by applying a base coat, polishing it, cutting a paper mask which is held tightly over the area to be covered, and airbrushing on the contrasting metal color.

While metalizers give a more bare-metal-like finish than aluminum enam-

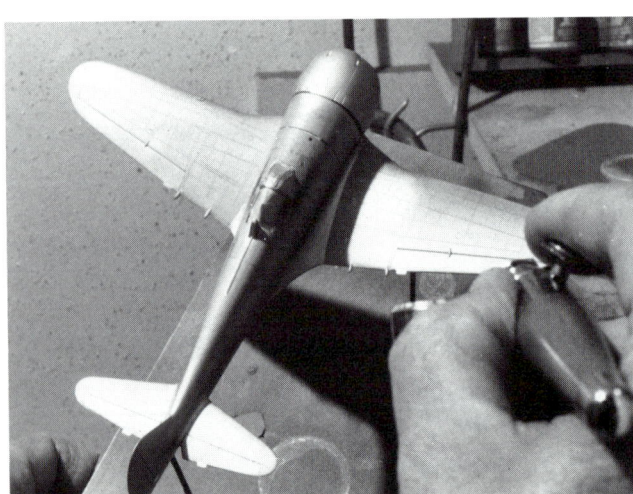
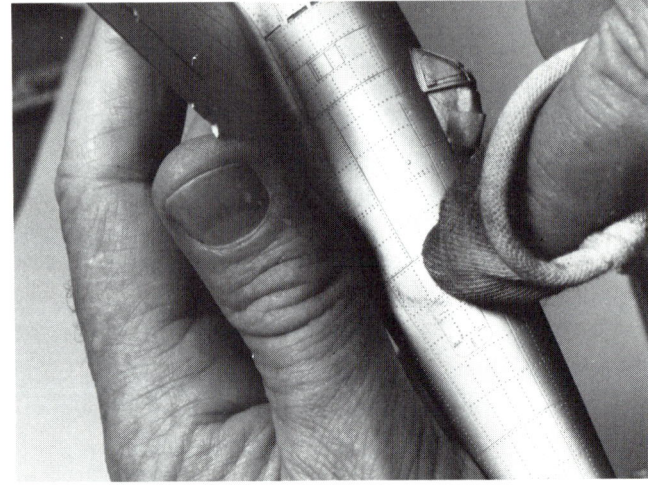

(Left) Airbrush Floquil Old Silver as you would any other color. Two light coats should be sufficient to cover. (Right) After letting the paint dry for 24 hours, buff Old Silver with a dab of toothpaste on a soft cloth to bring out the metallic shine.

When thoroughly dry, buffing gloss enamel with toothpaste yields a realistic aircraft finish, as on this 1/48 scale Testor Travel Air.

els, they have many of the same drawbacks. They can't be masked over with tape, so painted trim must be applied first and covered. They can be handled only with cloth or tissue, or else they'll show fingerprints.

Metalized finishes can be sealed, however, with their own special sealers. Sealers eliminate some of the handling problem, and will even allow gentle masking if you're brave enough. Unfortunately, sealers also dull the gleaming new bare-metal look, giving it a mildly oxidized appearance.

Floquil silvers. One group of products has none of the disadvantages of enamels and metalizers: Floquil silvers. These unique, lacquer-like model railroad paints come in three shades (Old Silver, Bright Silver, and Platinum Mist), spray on easily, dry hard, can be handled with no fear of fingerprints, and can be masked without fear of lifting. Dusted on in light coats, Floquil silvers can be applied over putty with no ill effects, and they won't attack the plastic. Best of all, they can be rubbed out with a mild, oil-based rubbing compound or toothpaste to the point that they look like slightly oxidized aluminum — just the ticket if you're into light weathering.

After the model is washed and dried, spray on Floquil silver in a light coat. One coat may do it, but apply no more than two. When the model is covered, stop; too much paint just increases the drying time.

Set the model aside for 24 hours, then rub off any moldy-appearing overspray using a tissue or soft cloth. This in itself will produce a shine. You may find this is all the polishing required to achieve the effect you want. If you want more shine, polish the finish with a tiny dab of toothpaste (not gel) on a lightly dampened cloth and wipe clean with another. (Don't use metal polish; the acid in it will take off the paint.)

For variations in panel shading, mask around appropriate panels and polish them "cross-grain" with rubbing compound. Rub too hard and make a hole in the finish? Just leave your masking in place, wash off the compound, and paint over the area. Polish it when dry; you'll get still another variation in shading.

It's possible to achieve at least three shades of aluminum by painting your model with a single Floquil silver color. By leaving the fabric control surfaces unpolished, they will look much like a doped finish. Polishing the airframe with toothpaste will give you a light shade of aluminum; polishing

(Left) Polish hard-to-reach areas with toothpaste on a cotton swab or bent pipe cleaner. Watch unprotected swab ends —

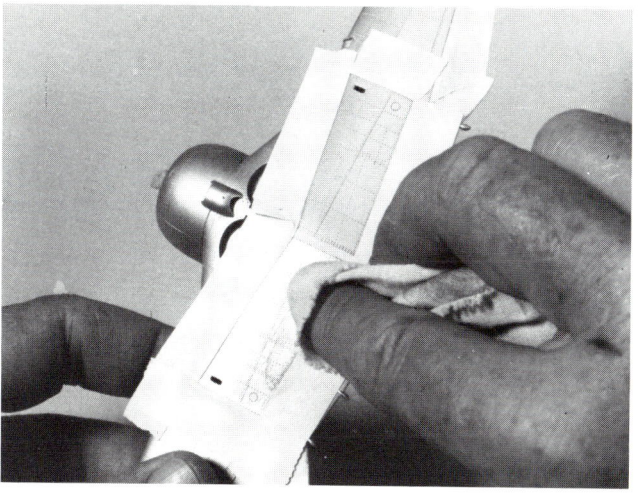

they scratch. (Right) To achieve a darker shade of aluminum, mask an area and polish it with fine rubbing compound.

Decals adhere tightly to this Ki-44 Tojo finished in Floquil Old Silver; no additional gloss coating was needed.

The decals on this AMT 1/48 scale Beechcraft Staggerwing adhered well to its glossy finish, but the borders of the markings had to be trimmed closely for a painted-on look.

gun bay covers, access hatches, and gasoline tank covers with rubbing compound will give you a darker shade.

The ability to mask over the aluminum means that you can paint on antiglare panels and markings after the metal finish is in place. Decals stick beautifully; trim them to the edge of their paint — no borders — for best effect.

Applying gloss enamel paint. Gloss enamels require the same careful base preparation as metalizers in terms of absolute freedom from scratches. Seams, however, can be cemented with liquid cement and putty can be used as a filler. The "secret" to top-notch results with a gloss enamel finish is fourfold.

First: Thin the paint properly. Most gloss enamels are thick; a ratio of at least one part thinner to one part paint is a must, and even more thinner may be required.

Second: Clean the model thoroughly. The airframe must be washed and completely free of dust.

Third: Spray on one coat at a time. Apply the paint just heavy enough to produce a shine immediately after a pass is made with the airbrush, and let it dry at least 24 hours before applying another coat. Between coats sand out any lint in the finish, then wash the model again.

Fourth: Rub out the paint. Once the model is thoroughly dry — give it at least a week — rub out the finish with toothpaste. This will kill the bright, toylike shine and give the model the look of a real aircraft.

Gloss enamel finishes can be masked over for application of other colors, but don't grasp the model in one spot for long while you're masking. Even dried gloss enamel is soft, and the heat of your hand can easily melt your fingerprints into the finish.

As with bare-metal finishes, you'll find that decals stick beautifully to gloss paints. Be sure to trim the markings to the edges of the painted areas.

This 1/48 scale Ki-100 Tony shows three distinct shades of aluminum: unbuffed control surfaces, toothpaste-buffed main body, and compound-buffed panels. All are Floquil Old Silver.

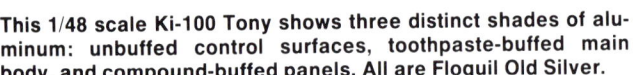

This simple diorama consists of a single war-weary Monogram 1/48 scale B-17 with three figures — pilot, copilot, and a ground crewman. The free-form base has been scored and painted to represent a concrete airfield apron.

12 Displaying your finished models

Showing off

When you've spent weeks — perhaps months — building a superdetailed and weathered model, one that you're particularly proud of, you probably won't be content to just let it sit on a tabletop or shelf to collect dust, fingerprints, and hard knocks. You'll want a display case to protect it from the elements, touchers, and carelessness.

If your model is small you should be able to buy a case for it at your hobby shop or through a mail order house. If your model is too big or the wrong shape for a ready-made case, you can build one. In fact, a clear plastic display cover is simpler to build than another model!

Building your own display covers. All cities, and most towns, have a plastic supply house of some sort (check your Yellow Pages). Most such shops will be happy to cut the plastic to the sizes you need for sides, ends, and top of your cover, and many will even cement it together for you, if you like.

If you have a power saw at home, you'll be money ahead if you buy cement — usually a stronger formulation of the same kind of liquid cement we use for models — and a sheet of clear acrylic plastic and cut it yourself. A band saw is particularly good for this, but a circular saw with a fine-tooth blade is almost as good. Once the pieces are cut, file and sand the saw marks off the edges.

To assemble the cover, hold an end and a side together at one corner and apply the cement with a draftsman's ruling pen or a pointed brush, letting capillary attraction draw the cement into the seam. Let the first corner set a few minutes, then work your way around the other three corners. Next, set your joined sides and ends upside down on the top and cement the top in place. Give the cemented seams time to dry, clean the cover with plastic cleaner, and you're ready to set it over your model.

You can stop here, if you like, for such a cover will afford the protection your model needs from dust and all but the hardest knocks. But the cover will look better with a bottom, one that will hold the top in place and provide a base for the model.

Making a plywood base. Bases cut from ¾" plywood work well. If you have a table saw you can bevel the

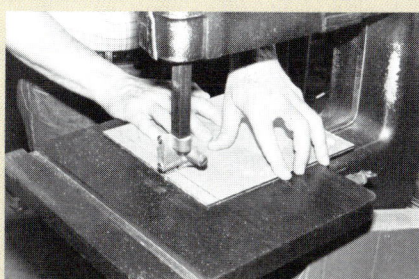  

(Left) Cutting the top and sides for a clear acrylic display cover with a band saw, (center) finishing the edges of the components with a file and sandpaper, and (right) assembling the case by holding the edges together and applying liquid cement.

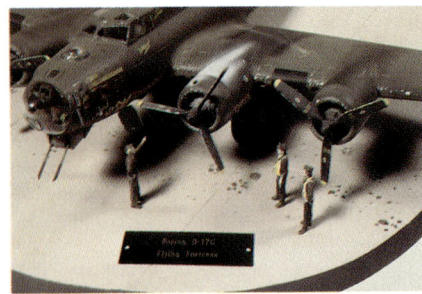

A close-up of the B-17 diorama reveals the crew chief and pilots talking over flak damage to an engine and propeller.

A base cut from plywood, stained, and covered with art paper completes a display case for this Travel Air Mystery Ship. An engraved nameplate adds the final touch.

edges and cut a groove around the top to retain the clear plastic cover, or you can trim the outside of the base with molding from a building supply store, creating the groove for the top by putting a thin spacer between the molding and the base.

If your base is good-quality wood, you may want to stain or varnish it, or both. If not, you can paint it or cover it with art paper in a color complementary to your plane. A final touch that adds a professional look is to have a nameplate made at a trophy house and place it inside the case to identify the plane — and you as its builder.

Dioramas. Once you've gotten into case making, you may want to take it one step farther, placing the plane in the setting in which it was (or is) used, thereby creating a diorama.

Begin by putting your plane on the right surface: a concrete ramp, crushed coral, or grass. Add mechanic and pilot figures to show how big the plane is and direct attention to a particular spot or feature of the model. You may also add support vehicles: bomb dollies, towing tractors, jeeps, gasoline trucks, and perhaps go so far as to add trees and buildings.

Unfortunately, most of the raw materials for dioramas are in 1/35 scale, the most popular size among armor modelers. But if you build 1/48 scale aircraft, take heart: O gauge model railroad equipment is also 1/48 scale, and many accessories are available in your hobby shop's model railroad department. With imagination and planning you can build a realistic diorama in any scale from whatever is at hand.

Diorama building and figure painting are arts unto themselves. Good books on both subjects are available at your hobby shop.

So now you know. So now you know what happened to the cracks. But that was a long time ago, when you first opened this book. Since then you've been introduced not only to techniques to keep the model's seams from showing, but to methods that enhance all aspects of construction, finishing, detailing, weathering, and displaying your models.

As you apply these techniques you'll find there's more to model building than just building models. The bottom line, really, is satisfaction. First you'll find satisfaction in the models you build simply because you know you do a good job. They look like scaled-down versions of the real things, and you're proud to put them on display.

You'll also gain a sense of artistic satisfaction from such a realistic creation. You may not think of yourself as an artist, but you should. You work with artist's tools — paints, brushes, airbrushes, and the like. And after a time, you'll find yourself developing a modeling style of your own, a style so artistically unique that your work can be recognized on sight by your peers, without you ever being present.

Of course, from the time you picked up your first kit you've been dealing with an art form: miniatures. And while miniature aircraft may not have the universal appeal of Peter Carl Fabergé's dioramas inside eggshells, they are nonetheless a part of the form. They portray a subject, and they have emotional appeal. Don't you think so? Just listen to the oohs and aahs of your fellow modelers next time you unveil a new masterpiece. If you're still not convinced, try presenting a model of a crusty old sky warrior's favorite combat plane to him sometime, and that should do it; you may move him to tears.

Finally, you'll gain satisfaction from the link with history that develops out of your model research. In a sense, all models are historic because they depict something that already exists. Airplanes have been around through two world wars, have taken part in many smaller conflicts, and have become an indispensable part of our civilian transportation system. If your interest lies in a particular era — World War One or World War Two or the "Golden Age," for example — eventually you'll end up surrounded, not only by many models, but by so much literature that you'll become the resident expert on the subject.

One side effect of your research may be more important in the long run than the facts you learn about aircraft. You may find that the activity the plane took part in was interesting enough to cause you to read further. If so, eventually you'll develop an understanding of the events of the past and the people who made them happen, people who have led us to where we stand today. It's been said that one of the reasons that men keep making the same mistakes is they fail to read the minutes of the last meeting. Through model building research you'll be reading those minutes. And maybe, just maybe, the greatest satisfaction of all will come from applying your understanding to help prevent the mistakes of the past from being repeated.

But more than likely all this satisfaction is in your future. You've probably read this book straight through and haven't built a model yet. So get your kit and your tools, and turn back to page one.

There is no end.